I0116857

Mind-Bending Trivia for Adults

Fascinating Facts and Quirky Knowledge Across History, Science, and Pop Culture For Fun Conversations and Quick Brain Workouts

Larry Solesbee

Albino Zucchini Studios

ISBN: 979-8-9925891-2-2 hardcover
ISBN 979-8-9925891-0-8 (eBook)
ISBN 979-8-9925891-1-5 (paperback)

Contents

Introduction   7

1. CHAPTER 1: POP CULTURE AND MODERN
   ODDITIES   11
   1.1 The Evolution of Internet Memes   13
   1.2 Surprising Facts About Iconic Movies   15
   1.3 The Weirdest World Records   18

2. CHAPTER 2: FOOD FACTS THAT WILL SURPRISE
   YOU   23
   2.1 Unusual Food Combinations That Work   26
   2.2 Strange Eating Habits from History   29
   2.3 Time-out for a Trivia matching quiz #1   31

3. CHAPTER 3: FASCINATING FIGURES AND
   RECORDS   35
   3.1 Unbelievable Animal Achievements   38
   3.2 Extraordinary Achievements in Science and
   Technology   40
   3.3 The rest of the story: Modems.   43

4. CHAPTER 4: GEOGRAPHY   47
   4.1 Trivia about Geographical Oddities Providing a
   Global Perspective   50

5. CHAPTER 5: NATURE'S MYSTERIES   57
   5.1 Mystical Forests and Their Secrets   60
   5.2 Puzzling Geological Formations   62
   5.3 Time-out: Here's a list of more than 40
   unbelievable facts   68

6. CHAPTER 6: LAWS AND CUSTOMS YOU WON'T
   BELIEVE   71
   6.1 Strange Festivities and Traditions   75
   6.2 Time-out for a Trivia matching quiz #2   80

7. CHAPTER 7: TIME TRAVEL AND SCI-FI WONDERS 83
7.1 Theories of Time Travel in Science 83
7.2 Sci-Fi Technologies That Became Reality 86
7.3 Iconic Sci-Fi Books and Their Predictions 88

8. CHAPTER 8: TECHNOLOGY AND THE FUTURE 95
8.1 Reflection Section: AI in Your Life 98
8.2 Breakthroughs in Space Travel 98
8.3 Here's a list of 50 common items invented or significantly popularized in the past 50 years, covering a range of technological, lifestyle, and everyday innovations: 101

9. CHAPTER 9: SCIENCE ODDITIES 103
9.1 The Mysteries of Dark Matter 108
9.2 Strange Scientific Experiments 110

10. CHAPTER 10: HISTORY'S HIDDEN GEMS 115
10.1 Secret Societies Throughout History 119
10.2 Little-Known Historical Events That Changed the World 122
10.3 Time-out for a Trivia matching quiz #3 126

11. CHAPTER 11: STRANGE SPORTS AND GAMES 129
11.1 The World of Extreme Ironing 129
11.2 Quirky Board Games from Around the Globe 131
11.3 Bizarre Olympic Events 134

12. CHAPTER 12: MIND-BLOWING MATH AND NUMBERS 139
12.1 Unsolved Mathematical Mysteries 142
12.2 Math in Nature: The Golden Ratio 144

13. CHAPTER 13: LANGUAGE AND WORDS YOU WON'T BELIEVE EXIST 149
13.1 Bonus list of words with bizarre meanings. 151
13.2 Did You Know These Things Had Names? 152
13.3 Untranslatable Words from Other Cultures 154
13.4 The Evolution of Slang Over Time 156

14. CHAPTER 14: MIND-BOGGLING COINCIDENCES   161

     14.1 Historical Coincidences That Defy Explanation   161

     14.2 Unbelievable Personal Stories of Coincidence   164

     14.3 The Science Behind Coincidences   166

     Conclusion   171

     Index   175

     References   191

Introduction

Ever wonder why in Switzerland it is illegal to own just one guinea pig? No, it's not because the Swiss have a particular vendetta against single guinea pigs. This quirky law exists because guinea pigs are social creatures, and leaving one alone is considered animal abuse. It's odd, fascinating, and precisely the kind of delightful nugget of knowledge that will make you the star of your next dinner party.

Welcome to "Mind-Bending Trivia for Adults: Fascinating Facts and Quirky Knowledge for Fun Conversations and Quick Brain Workouts." This book's purpose is simple: to entertain, educate, and arm you with a treasure trove of facts that will make your friends marvel at your vast repository of trivia. Think of it as your

personal arsenal for sparking lively conversations and giving your brain a quick workout.

The vision here is to take trivia beyond the realm of dry facts. We aim to present each tidbit with a splash of humor and a dash of quirkiness. You won't just learn that the heart of a shrimp is located in its head; you'll be challenged to guess where it is before we reveal the answer. This book is designed to make learning fun and engaging, transforming the mundane into the extraordinary.

Who is this book for? If you're an adult with a curious mind, someone who loves learning new things, or if you enjoy using trivia to connect with others, you've picked up the right book. It's perfect for those who want to keep their minds sharp and have a repertoire of fascinating tidbits ready to share. Whether you're trying to impress at a social gathering or just want a mental workout, this book has got you covered.

Let's take a quick tour of the themed sections awaiting you. We have chapters on Pop Culture and Modern Oddities, where you'll find out why a broken piano was once the most popular instrument in American homes. In Food Facts That Will Surprise You, discover how honey never spoils, making it the edible version of a time capsule. Fascinating Figures and Records will introduce you to the world's quirkiest achievements. Geography and Nature's Mysteries will make you question everything you know about the natural world. And for those who love a good paradox, Mind-Boggling Coincidences will leave you scratching your head.

A little about me: Besides puns, literalisms and dad jokes, I'm a trivia enthusiast with some ideas for spicing up everyday conversations. I believe that trivia is one of the solutions to monotony and that a well-placed fact can transform any gathering into a lively discussion. My appreciation for quirky and humorous descriptions makes entertaining facts accessible to everyone, ensuring that you walk away with both a smile and newfound knowledge.

So, dear reader, I invite you to dive into this world of mind-bending trivia. Explore the pages, challenge your knowledge, and share these fascinating facts with friends and family. Whether reading for fun or sharpening your mind, each page holds a surprise waiting to be uncovered. Let's get started—you never know what you might learn next!

1

Chapter 1: Pop Culture and Modern Oddities

Did you know that the phrase "Netflix and chill" started as a literal invitation to binge-watch TV shows and relax, and evolved into a euphemism for something entirely different? This transformation, much like a caterpillar morphing into a butterfly, perfectly encapsulates the quirky, ever-evolving realm of pop culture and modern oddities. Welcome to a chapter where the bizarre is the norm, and the ordinary is anything but. From the curious evolution of the internet meme to the strange laws governing pet guinea pigs, this chapter promises to take you on a delightful romp through the unexpected twists and turns of modern life. Whether you're a trivia aficionado or a casual consumer of quirky knowledge, prepare to be entertained and perhaps even a little bewildered.

The notion that broken pianos were once a staple in American homes captures a fascinating slice of history. In the late 19th and early 20th centuries, pianos were more than musical instruments; they were symbols of middle-class status and cultural refinement. With the advent of the Industrial Revolution, pianos became more affordable, leading to widespread ownership. However, as technology marched forward, these beloved instruments often fell into disrepair. Rather than being discarded, many were repurposed into furniture or kept as decorative pieces, serving as nostalgic reminders of a bygone era. This transition from cherished instrument to quirky household artifact reflects the broader societal shift from acoustic to electronic forms of entertainment, marking the end of the piano's reign as the heart of family entertainment.

In Switzerland, it is illegal to own just one guinea pig because they are social animals that need companionship to avoid loneliness and distress. The Swiss Animal Protection Law classifies guinea pigs as *"social creatures,"* meaning they naturally live in groups and require interaction with their own kind for mental well-being. Owning a single guinea pig is seen as a form of animal cruelty due to the negative impact on their psychological health.

The law reflects Switzerland's strict and progressive animal welfare regulations, which emphasize the importance of catering to the social needs of animals. This requirement is similar for other social pets, like rabbits, to ensure they have a suitable quality of life. There are even rental services in Switzerland that offer temporary companionship if one guinea pig dies, so the remaining one isn't left alone until a permanent solution is found.

1.1 The Evolution of Internet Memes

Dive deep into the vibrant, whimsical universe of internet memes, those ephemeral shards of digital culture that propagate with the swiftness of wildfire. The concept of the "meme" was first coined by Richard Dawkins in his seminal 1976 work, "The Selfish Gene," as a framework for understanding how cultural information proliferates. Yet, the journey from this academic inception to the internet meme's current incarnation is nothing short of remarkable. It began with the "Dancing Baby" in the late 1990s, a crudely animated figure that gyrated its way into our collective digital consciousness, marking the dawn of meme culture. Hot on its heels, the "Hamster Dance" meme, with its infectious melody, had us unwittingly nodding along, pondering the mysterious allure of these simple yet captivating creations. As the digital landscape evolved, so too did the ecosystem of meme culture. Initial platforms like 4chan and Reddit emerged as fertile grounds for the birth and proliferation of memes, acting as incubators for viral content. This ecosystem expanded with the advent of Facebook, Instagram, and TikTok, elevating memes from internet novelties to staples of digital communication and expressions of social currency. YouTube's unending cascade of viral videos further cemented memes within the mainstream, creating a self-sustaining cycle of consumption and creation that delighted digital natives and newcomers alike. More recently, each of the social media platforms has embraced the "reels" showing a wide range of topics in video form.

Certain memes have risen above the digital fray to become icons of popular culture. Grumpy Cat, with its eternally discontented visage, spawned countless memes, merchandising deals, and even a movie, proving the unique ability of memes to transcend digital boundaries. "Rickrolling" redefined internet pranks, embedding Rick Astley's 1987 hit "Never Gonna Give You Up" into the fabric of online culture. The "Distracted Boyfriend" meme became a canvas for exploring themes of fidelity, desire, and the human condition, while "Pepe the Frog" illustrated the darker side of memes, becoming embroiled in political controversy and symbolizing the complex interplay between internet culture and real-world ideologies. "Woman yelling at a cat" is an Internet meme first used in a post in 2019. It shows two images: on the left, a screen capture from an episode of The Real Housewives of Beverly Hills, depicting cast member crying and pointing and a picture depicting a cat named Smudge, sitting at a dinner table with a seemingly bemused expression. Over time many posters swapped in people currently in the news and or various situations with the cat, changing the text to fit. For example, Bernie, next paragraph, wearing mittens holding the cat.

Memes have matured from their humble beginnings into powerful instruments of social critique and political discourse. "Bernie Sanders' Mittens" (2021). During President Biden's inauguration, an image of Bernie Sanders sitting cross-legged in a parka and distinctive mittens became a viral meme. It was quickly photoshopped into countless scenarios, becoming a symbol of cozy practicality and nonchalance. In the realm of politics, memes wield influence comparable to traditional media, shaping narratives, influencing public opinion, and mobilizing voter turnout with their incisive humor and accessibility. They serve as the digital era's satire, skewering societal norms and political figures with equal fervor. The COVID-19 pandemic underscored the unifying power of memes, offering solace and a shared sense of humor amidst the upheaval, and illustrating their role not just as vehicles of entertainment, but as essential threads in the fabric of contemporary culture.

Whether you're a seasoned meme connoisseur or just dipping your toes into the meme pool, remember that memes are not just frivolous images. They are cultural artifacts, a snapshot of our collective consciousness, and a testament to the creativity and humor of the human spirit. So next time you encounter a meme, embrace its absurdity, appreciate its wit, and perhaps even join in the fun of creating your own.

1.2 Surprising Facts About Iconic Movies

Ah, the magic of Hollywood, where the line between fiction and reality blurs like a poorly focused camera lens. Take "Poltergeist," for instance, a film that famously used real skeletons during its chilling pool scene. Why real skeletons? Apparently, they were cheaper than fake ones, turning the set into a veritable house of horrors for the actors involved. And then there's "The Shining," where Jack Nicholson's now-iconic "Here's Johnny!" was completely improvised. Nicholson's ax-wielding improvisation added an extra layer of horror that left audiences gripping their popcorn in terror. Further, The hexagonal carpet pattern from the Overlook

Hotel in *The Shining* was recreated in *Toy Story* (1995) in the hallway of Sid's house. Meanwhile, the saga of Darth Vader is a tale of multiple personas. David Prowse provided the imposing physique, while James Earl Jones lent his booming voice. And let's not forget about the uncredited Sebastian Shaw, who played the unmasked Vader in "Return of the Jedi." It's as if Hollywood decided one actor wasn't enough to capture the complexity of the galaxy's most notorious villain.

When it comes to inspiration, reality often weaves its way into the fantastical. "The Exorcist," for instance, drew from the chilling real-life exorcism of Roland Doe, a story that sent shivers down the spine of anyone brave enough to hear it. As for "Inception," Christopher Nolan's mind-bending masterpiece was born from the ethereal world of dreams. Nolan, inspired by his own dreams, crafted a narrative that left viewers questioning the nature of reality. Then there's "Jurassic Park," where Michael Crichton's fascination with cloning and genetic engineering collided with the allure of dinosaurs. His curiosity gave rise to a film that roared its way into the annals of cinematic legend. The sounds for the dinosaurs in *Jurassic Park* were created using a mix of various animal noises. For instance, the T. rex's roar was a combination of a baby elephant, a tiger, and an alligator. Originally, the script for *Back to the Future* had the time machine as a refrigerator, not a DeLorean. However, it was changed due to concerns that children might imitate the movie and accidentally trap themselves inside fridges.

Casting decisions are where Hollywood dreams and "what ifs" collide. Imagine Tom Selleck as Indiana Jones, his mustache braving the treacherous world of ancient relics instead of

Magnum P.I.'s Hawaiian shirts. The role, as we know, went to Harrison Ford, but the mere thought of Selleck donning the iconic fedora is enough to spark a parallel universe of cinematic speculation. In another alternate reality, Will Smith could have been Neo in "The Matrix," dodging bullets with the same flair he brought to "Men in Black." But Smith passed on the role, leaving Keanu Reeves to redefine cool with his stoic demeanor and effortless charm. Emily Blunt, too, was considered for the role of Black Widow in the Marvel Cinematic Universe, a role that Scarlett Johansson ultimately made her own.

The cultural impact of iconic films is undeniable. "The Matrix" revolutionized modern sci-fi and action films, introducing groundbreaking effects and a philosophical narrative that left audiences pondering their existence. Its "bullet time" sequences became the benchmark for action choreography, influencing countless films and video games. Keanu Reeves underwent four months of intense martial arts training to prepare for his role as Neo. The iconic fight scenes were performed without using stunt doubles, adding authenticity to the film. Despite being the film's iconic character, In "The Terminator," Arnold Schwarzenegger only has 17 lines of dialogue in the entire movie. He famously says, "I'll be back," which became a legendary catchphrase. Meanwhile, "The Godfather" reshaped American cinema, offering a gritty depiction of organized crime that remains a touchstone for filmmakers. Its influence is so profound that phrases like "an offer you can't refuse" have seeped into everyday language, a testament to its enduring legacy.

"Titanic" sailed into theaters and shattered box office records, its love story set against the backdrop of disaster capturing the hearts of millions. The film catapulted Leonardo DiCaprio and Kate Winslet into superstardom, and for better or worse, Celine Dion's "My Heart Will Go On" became an anthem for romantic tragedy. During the filming of *Titanic*, more than 80 crew members, including James Cameron, were hospitalized after someone spiked the lobster chowder with PCP (a hallucinogenic drug). The culprit was never found, and it remains a mystery.

And who could forget "The Lion King"? This animated classic's tale of loss, redemption, and a lion cub's quest for identity has resonated across generations. Its unforgettable soundtrack and vibrant animation have cemented its place in the pantheon of Disney's greatest hits. In "E.T. the Extra-Terrestrial", The filmmakers originally approached M&M's for a product placement deal, but they declined. Instead, they used Reese's Pieces, which led to a 65% increase in the candy's sales after the movie's release. Films like these entertain and shape our culture, influence our conversations, and leave us with indelible memories that transcend the screen.

1.3 The Weirdest World Records

In a world where the ordinary often feels mundane, it's a relief to know that some people dedicate their lives to the extraordinary—like spinning a basketball on a toothbrush, 1 minute and 47.4 seconds. Yes, that's an actual record, and while most of us struggle to keep a basketball spinning on our fingers for a few seconds, someone out there has perfected this bizarre art. Then there's the marathon runner who decided that finishing 26.2 miles wasn't challenging enough without donning a full-body animal costume. Imagine crossing the finish line with both sore muscles and a furry suit that smells like a zoo on a hot summer day. It's safe to say these individuals have a knack for endurance that borders on the absurd.

Speaking of endurance, let's not forget the romantic (or perhaps masochistic) souls who set the record for the longest continuous kiss, 58 hours, 35 minutes, and 58 seconds. After hours of lip-locking, they were probably more relieved to part ways than to set a world record. And then there's the ink aficionado who managed to get the most tattoos in 24 hours. This feat requires not just endurance but also a high pain threshold and, presumably, a tattoo artist with a steady hand and a lot of caffeine. These records make you question the limits of human endurance and the lengths people will go to etch their names into the history books.

If tattoos and toothbrushes aren't your thing, perhaps odd collections are more your speed. Take, for instance, the largest collection of rubber ducks, which quacks in at over 9,000 pieces. Imagine the sea of yellow, a veritable tsunami of squeaky toys, each with its own unique charm. Then there's the most extensive collection of "Star Wars" memorabilia, housing everything from lightsabers to life-size Wookiees. It's a testament to a galaxy far, far away taking up a very real space in someone's home. And for those with a penchant for the whimsical, there's the largest collection of garden gnomes, over 2,000, a gathering of bearded little men that could easily populate an entire mythical village.

But not all collections are as charming. Enter the realm of nail clippings. Yes, someone decided that collecting these keratinous crescents was a worthy pursuit. Whether it's for a science experiment or just a quirky hobby, it certainly makes for a unique conversation starter. These collections show us that one person's trash is indeed another's treasure, and the world is a more interesting place for it.

Moving on to the culinary realm, the food records are as jaw-dropping as they are stomach-churning. The largest pizza ever created could easily feed a small nation, (details next chapter), while competitive eaters push the boundaries of human consumption with feats like devouring the most hot dogs in ten minutes. And let's not overlook the largest scoop of ice cream ever served—an indulgence that could satisfy even the most insatiable sweet tooth. (details next chapter) If that's not enough, there's the record for the longest line of sandwiches, a veritable carb-load stretching as far as the eye can see.

Animals, too, have their claim to fame with records that range from the adorable to the astonishing. There's the longest cat whiskers, 19 centimeters (7.5 inches), a Guinness Record, but 30.5 centimeters (12 inches), has not been verified, a feature that surely makes its owner feel like the feline version of a wise old wizard. The dog with the longest ears, 34 centimeters (13.38 inches), could easily double as a blanket, while the fastest tortoise, 0.28 meters per second (0.92 feet per second), defies expectations with its impressive speed. And who could forget the largest gathering of people dressed as penguins, 972, a scene that would make even the most stoic Antarctic bird crack a smile?

These records remind us that the world is full of surprises, and human (and animal) creativity knows no bounds. Whether it's through feats of endurance, quirky collections, or epicurean extravaganzas, these records push the envelope of what's possible. They inspire us to look at the world through a lens of wonder and curiosity, proving that even the strangest pursuits can lead to greatness. So, whether you're spinning a basketball on a toothbrush or collecting garden gnomes, remember that the weirdest records are often the most memorable.

2

Chapter 2: Food Facts That Will Surprise You

Imagine a world where pizza didn't exist. I know—it's a horror story worthy of a Stephen King novel. But fear not, because pizza is very much real and has a history as rich as a gooey cheese pull. Our culinary journey starts with the flatbreads of ancient Egypt and Greece, where people had the ingenious idea to slap various toppings onto dough. Fast forward to Naples, Italy, the birthplace of modern pizza, where a baker named Raffaele Esposito whipped up a pie in 1889 to honor Queen Margherita of Savoy. He topped it with tomatoes, mozzarella, and basil to represent the Italian flag. Talk about patriotism with a side of carbs! This creation was so revolutionary that it not only pleased the queen but also set the stage for pizza to conquer the world. Soon, regional variations emerged, like New York-style pizza with its

foldable slices and Chicago's deep-dish pizza, which is more of a cheesy, saucy casserole masquerading as a pie. Each style claims superiority, sparking debates that threaten friendships and family gatherings alike.

The largest pizza ever created measured an incredible 1,296.72 square meters (13,990 square feet). It was made in Los Angeles, California, on January 19, 2023, as a collaboration between YouTube content creator Airrack and Pizza Hut. The project used over 13,653 pounds of dough, nearly 5,000 pounds of marinara sauce, 8,800 pounds of cheese, and around 630,496 pepperoni slices. The pizza was baked in sections at the Los Angeles Convention Center and then donated to local charities to prevent food waste.

The largest scoop of ice cream ever served weighed 3,010 pounds (1,365.31 kg). It was created by Kemps Dairy in Cedarburg, Wisconsin, in 2014 as part of their 100th anniversary celebration. The flavor was strawberry, and the scoop required the skills of five professional snow sculptors to shape it. The massive ice cream scoop was equivalent to about 733 regular containers of ice cream. Following the unveiling, the scoop was shared with thousands of attendees at the Cedarburg Strawberry Festival.

Now, let's turn our attention to another beloved treat: chocolate. This delightful confection has a history as rich as its flavor. The Olmecs of southern Mexico were likely the first to ferment, roast, and grind cacao beans, crafting a bitter drink that was less Willy Wonka and more Mayan ceremonial brew. The Maya and Aztecs revered cacao, using it in rituals and as currency, long before it became the sweet treat we know today. When Spanish explorers introduced chocolate to Europe, it was a game-changer. The Europeans, with their penchant for sugar, transformed the bitter concoction into a decadent delight. Enter Daniel Peter, who in the late 19th century, added milk to chocolate, giving birth to milk chocolate and making him a hero to sweet tooths everywhere. Joseph Fry followed suit with the invention of the chocolate bar, because who doesn't want their chocolate in a handy, portable form? Today, chocolate is a global industry with brands like Hershey's and Cadbury vying for a spot in your candy stash, proving that the world runs on cocoa and sugar.

And of course, we can't talk about iconic foods without mentioning the hamburger, a staple of American cuisine that has its roots in Hamburg, Germany. The hamburger steak, a simple patty of ground beef, was a hit among the Hamburg seafaring community before it made its way to the United States. The 1904 St. Louis World's Fair marked a pivotal moment when the hamburger, as we know it, was introduced to the masses. Fast food chains like McDonald's and Burger King took this humble patty and turned it into a global sensation, creating an empire built on sesame seed buns and secret sauces. But let's not forget Wendy's, which decided that round was too mainstream and introduced the square hamburger. Because why not? In today's culinary landscape, burgers have evolved into gourmet masterpieces, with chefs experimenting with everything from truffle aioli to plant-based patties. It's a burger bonanza, and everyone's invited.

So, what's the takeaway from these tasty tales? Whether it's pizza, ice cream, chocolate, or hamburgers, these foods have not only shaped our palates but also our culture. They remind us that food is more than sustenance—it's history, creativity, and sometimes a heated debate over which pizza style reigns supreme. Next time you bite into a slice, lick an ice cream cone, savor a square of chocolate, or chomp down on a burger, remember the stories and the journey each has taken to delight your taste buds. And maybe, just maybe, you'll find yourself sharing these flavorful facts at your next dinner party, leaving your friends both impressed and hungry for more.

2.1 Unusual Food Combinations That Work

Picture this: a spoonful of creamy peanut butter perched atop a crunchy pickle slice. If you're raising an eyebrow right now, you're not alone. This peculiar pairing might sound like the result of a culinary dare gone too far, but hear me out. The salty richness of peanut butter perfectly complements the tangy zest of pickles, creating a mouthful of contrasting flavors that somehow, against all odds, balance each other out. It's a bit like a culinary odd couple sitcom, where opposites attract, creating a surprising harmony that keeps your taste buds guessing. This combination gained popularity during the Great Depression when folks had to get creative with limited ingredients. Pickles were cheap, peanut butter was a protein-packed staple, and together, they made a satisfying snack that proved necessity truly is the mother of invention.

Somehow, this reminds me of making peanut butter and mayonnaise sandwiches as a kid in the 1950s. And every time since then, thinking about that combination, I haven't had the guts to ever try it again.

Next, we have bacon and maple syrup—a duo that makes breakfast lovers everywhere swoon. Bacon, with its crispy, savory, umami-rich allure, meets the sticky, sweet embrace of maple syrup, and together they create a flavor profile that's nothing short of ambrosial. This sweet and salty symphony has become a hallmark of North American breakfasts, transcending its humble pancake accompaniment to inspire culinary creations like bacon-wrapped maple-glazed donuts. Yes, you read that right: a donut wrapped in bacon and drizzled with syrup. This pairing is proof that sometimes the best things in life are those that shouldn't work but do, like wearing socks with sandals or singing in the shower despite your dog's protests. It's a testament to the fact that breakfast is the most important meal of the day—especially when it involves bacon and syrup.

Then there's the delightful pairing of cheese and honey, a combination that will make your taste buds sing as if they've discovered an opera in a single bite. The savory, sometimes sharp notes of cheese find a perfect counterpoint in the smooth sweetness of honey, creating a balance that's both sophisticated and indulgent. Goat cheese paired with acacia honey is a classic combination that elevates any cheese platter, turning a simple snack into a gourmet experience. This pairing has been gracing cheese boards at fancy gatherings and potluck parties alike, making even the humblest of get-togethers feel like a Michelin-starred event. Cheese and honey prove that opposites not only attract but can also create culinary magic, making them the power couple of the appetizer world. Side-note: Honey never spoils, making it the edible version of a time capsule.

Finally, let's talk about chocolate and chili—a spicy twist that's been heating up palates since the days of the ancient Mesoamericans. The Aztecs and Maya knew a thing or two about flavor, and they weren't afraid to add a little heat to their cacao drinks. This bold combination has experienced a modern resurgence, finding its way into gourmet chocolate bars and culinary creations like mole sauce. Chocolate and chili are the culinary equivalent of a fiery tango, each enhancing the other's intensity and depth. Whether you're biting into a chili-infused chocolate bar or savoring a rich mole sauce over chicken, you'll find that the heat of the chili brings out the natural sweetness of the chocolate, creating a complex and exhilarating taste experience that's anything but ordinary.

These unusual food combinations remind us that sometimes the most unexpected pairings can bring the most delightful surprises. Whether you're exploring the salty-sweet wonders of bacon and maple syrup or the spicy allure of chocolate and chili, these pairings challenge our preconceptions and invite us to expand our culinary horizons. They prove that food is not just about sustenance—it's about adventure, creativity, and sometimes a little bit of daring. So next time you find yourself reaching for the pickles and peanut butter, remember that you're not just making a snack—you're embracing a delicious piece of history and a testament to the curious nature of the human palate.

2.2 Strange Eating Habits from History

When it comes to peculiar eating habits, the ancient Romans had a penchant for extravagance that would make even the most seasoned foodie raise an eyebrow. Imagine reclining on a cushioned chaise, surrounded by opulence, as you partake in a feast that lasts hours and includes delicacies like stuffed dormice and flamingo tongues. These lavish banquets weren't just about the food; they were a statement of wealth and status, each course an opportunity to flaunt one's affluence. The concept of the "vomitorium" often gets misunderstood as a room where Romans purged to make room for more food. In reality, vomitoria were passageways in amphitheaters, but the image of Romans overindulging to the point of excess isn't entirely far-fetched. These feasts were a celebration of life and a display of culinary creativity, where the more exotic the dish, the better. It was a time when gastronomy and gluttony danced a fine line, and the Romans relished every bite.

Fast forward to the medieval period, when banquets became a theatrical display of culinary art. Medieval feasts were not only about feeding the body but also the eyes and imagination. Illusion foods were the stars of these gatherings, with chefs crafting meat to look like fruit or creating intricate sugar sculptures that defied the boundaries of confectionery. Spices imported from distant lands added an air of mystery and sophistication to the dishes, while the presentation of food became an elaborate performance designed to impress and awe guests. These feasts held great social and political significance, often serving as the backdrop for alliances and negotiations. Imagine sitting at a long wooden table, the aroma of roasted meats mingling with the scent of cloves and cinnamon, as a lord and his subjects share a meal that is as much about spectacle as it is about sustenance. The medieval banquet was a stage where food told stories, and every bite was a chapter in the grand narrative of nobility and power.

The Victorian era brought its brand of quirky food trends, where gelatin molds and aspics reigned supreme. A Victorian dinner party wasn't complete without a wobbly tower of gelatinous delight, often encasing meats or vegetables in a translucent, quivering dome. The Victorians had a fascination with the exotic, and fruits like pineapples were a symbol of wealth and prestige, sometimes hired as centerpieces rather than served. This era also saw the rise of vegetarianism and health foods, with graham crackers and cornflakes making their debut as part of a movement towards diet reform. It was a time when food became a reflection of societal values, a testament to the complex relationship between culinary innovation and cultural aspiration. Imagine a table adorned with gelatin masterpieces, each wobble a testament to the Victorian pursuit of novelty and refinement, while guests sip on tea and discuss the merits of a meatless diet. It was a time when food was a medium for expression, and even a simple cracker could make a statement.

World War II introduced an era of rationing that demanded culinary creativity and ingenuity. As ingredients became scarce, home cooks rose to the challenge, transforming limited supplies into satisfying meals. Substitutes like powdered eggs and margarine became staples, while recipes like mock apple pie—made with Ritz crackers instead of apples—highlighted the resourcefulness of the time. Wartime cookbooks offered guidance on stretching ingredients and minimizing waste, turning meals into a testament to resilience and adaptability. Imagine gathering around a modest table, the air filled with the aroma of a meal born from necessity, where each bite is a reminder of the strength and perseverance that defines the human spirit. Wartime cooking was more than just sustenance; it was a symbol of unity and determination, a culinary testament to the adage that necessity is indeed the mother of invention.

These strange eating habits from history remind us that food is more than just nourishment; it's a reflection of culture, society, and the human experience. Whether through the opulence of Roman banquets, the theatricality of medieval feasts, the eccentricity of Victorian trends, or the ingenuity of wartime recipes, our relationship with food has always been intertwined with our history. As we transition to our next chapter, we'll explore how these historical influences continue to shape our modern culinary landscape.

2.3 Time-out for a Trivia matching quiz #1

Bizarre Words: Can you match these words to their descriptions below?

A- aglet

B- agraffe

C- armscye

D- Brannock device

E- box tent

F- columella nas

G- crapulence

H- dysania

I- glabella

J- griffonage

K- interrobang

L- minimus

M- overmorrow

N- petrichor

O- phosphenes

P- tines

Q- tittle

R- vagitus

S- vocables

T- wamble

1- armhole in clothes, where the sleeves are sewn

2- the condition of finding it difficult to get out of bed in the morning

3- the cry of a newborn baby

4- day after tomorrow

5- dot over an "i" or a "j"

6- Illegible hand-writing

7- a metallic device used to measure your feet at the shoe store

8- 'na na na' and 'la la la', which don't really have any meaning in the lyrics of any song

9- plastic or metallic coating at the end of your shoelaces

10- prongs on a fork

11- rumbling of stomach

12- sheen or light that you see when you close your eyes and press your hands on them

13- space between your eyebrows

14- space between your nostrils

15- That utterly sick feeling you get after eating or drinking too much

16- tiny plastic table placed in the middle of a pizza box

17- the way it smells after the rain

18- When you combine an exclamation mark with a question mark (like this ?!)

19- a wired cage that holds the cork in a bottle of champagne

20- Your tiny toe or finger

Trivia matching quiz answers

1-C, 2-H, 3-R, 4-M, 5-Q, 6-J, 7-D, 8-S, 9-A, 10-P, 11-T, 12-O, 13-I, 14-F, 15-G, 16-E, 17-N, 18-K, 19-B, 20-L

Trivia matching quiz chart in Chapter 13.2

3

Chapter 3: Fascinating Figures and Records

In a world where most of us struggle to make it to the gym three times a week, there exists a group of individuals who redefine the limits of human capability. These are the people who look at a marathon and think, "Why stop at one? Let's do fifty!" Such is the case with Dean Karnazes, a man who decided that running 50 marathons in 50 days across 50 states was a perfectly sane idea. While most of us would struggle to run to the fridge during commercial breaks, Karnazes powered through each grueling mile with the tenacity of a caffeinated squirrel. His feat leaves you wondering if he has some kind of secret fuel or if he's just the ultimate testament to human endurance—or perhaps both.

Then there's Benoît Lecomte, a man who looked at the Atlantic Ocean and thought, "I could swim across that." And swim he did, covering over 3,716 miles in 73 days in 1998, albeit with some rest on a sailboat because, let's face it, even superheroes need a nap sometimes. While this isn't officially recognized by Guinness, the sheer audacity of the attempt is enough to make you reconsider your own fitness goals. Not content with a single ocean, Lecomte also attempted the Pacific, making it 1,700 miles before pesky things like sail damage forced a halt. The oceans, it seems, are his version of a backyard pool.

Alex Honnold, another remarkable name, decided that climbing the 3,000-foot granite face of El Capitan without ropes would be a fun afternoon activity. Free solo climbing isn't for the faint of heart—or those with a fear of heights—but Honnold's ascent was a masterclass in focus and fear management. While most of us would need a change of pants just thinking about it, Honnold's calm demeanor as he scaled sheer rock is a testament to the power of the human mind over fear, or perhaps just a complete disregard for gravity.

Switching gears to feats of raw strength, we have Hafthor Bjornsson, who quite literally put the world on his shoulders by deadlifting 1,104 pounds. That's roughly the weight of a polar bear, a small car, or a particularly hefty family of four. While most of us grunt lifting a suitcase onto a luggage rack, Bjornsson's accomplishment makes you wonder if he moonlights as a superhero. Julius Maddox too has etched his name in the annals of strength, bench pressing more than many of us weigh—over 700 pounds, in fact. His record is a powerful reminder that with great strength comes, well, a really impressive Instagram following.

And let's not forget about Eamonn Keane, who thought lifting a cumulative weight of 1.1 million pounds in an hour was a fun way to spend an afternoon. Keane's record is a nod to both strength and stamina, making those of us who struggle with a single set of dumbbells rethink our life choices. Robert Wadlow, meanwhile, didn't have to lift a finger—or anything else—to make headlines. Standing at a staggering 8 feet 11 inches, Wadlow was a giant among men in the most literal sense, his height remaining unmatched to this day.

But physical prowess isn't the only realm where humans excel. Mental feats are equally mind-boggling. Take Alex Mullen, who can memorize a deck of cards faster than you can say "52 card pickup." And then there's Suresh Kumar Sharma, who recited over 70,000 digits of pi, a number so endless it makes infinity seem concise. Meanwhile, Michael Kearney earned a PhD at age 10, making the rest of us wonder what we're doing with our lives. Add to that Feliks Zemdegs, who solves Rubik's Cubes in mere seconds, reminding us that sometimes it's what's inside your head that packs the most punch.

Of course, the human spirit also loves a bit of whimsy, and nowhere is this more evident than in the realm of quirky records. Hollis Cantrell, for instance, holds the record for the most tattoos in 24 hours, turning his skin into a canvas of ink and endurance. Ashrita Furman, a jack-of-all-trades in the world of records, once balanced a lawnmower on his chin just because he could. Then there's Dalibor Jablanovic, who balanced 79 spoons on his body, a record that seems both impressive and oddly specific. And let's not forget Sanath Bandara, who wore 257 T-shirts at once, likely making him both the warmest and most stylish person in the room.

In the grand tapestry of human achievement, these records remind us that we're capable of extraordinary things, whether it's through sheer physical strength, mental agility, or whimsical creativity.

3.1 Unbelievable Animal Achievements

In the animal kingdom, speed is not just a concept; it's a life-or-death reality, and there's no better poster child for this than the cheetah. With a top speed of 70 miles per hour, cheetahs are the Formula 1 cars of the savanna. Their bodies are built for speed with a lightweight frame, long legs, and a tail that acts like a rudder to make those sharp turns while chasing down dinner. It's like watching a high-speed chase scene in a nature documentary, except the cheetahs don't have to worry about running out of gas. Meanwhile, in the skies, the grey-headed albatross holds court as the fastest bird in level flight, soaring at speeds of up to 79 miles per hour. With wingspans that stretch over 7 feet, these avian speedsters glide effortlessly, making the most of oceanic winds as they travel vast distances. It's as if they were born with a map and a jet engine, leaving other birds in their wake. Not to be outdone, the black marlin speeds through the ocean at a breakneck 82 miles per hour, slicing through the water with the precision of a torpedo. And then there's the dragonfly, an insect so agile it could moonlight as a tiny, aerial acrobat, darting and diving with astonishing accuracy.

Strength in the animal kingdom often comes in surprising packages. Take the dung beetle, for instance. While it might not be the most glamorous of creatures, it boasts an incredible claim to fame: the ability to lift 1,141 times its own body weight. That's like you carrying a dozen elephants on your back, all while rolling a ball of dung across the savanna. Talk about multitasking! Meanwhile, the Arctic tern embarks on the longest migration known, traveling over 44,000 miles from pole to pole each year. This tiny bird's endurance is unmatched, and it probably racks up more frequent flyer miles than any human could dream of. Then there's the tardigrade, or "water bear," which isn't much to look at but can survive extreme conditions that would make Rambo weep. Whether it's the vacuum of space or the fiery depths of a volcano, the tardigrade just shrugs it off, proving that size doesn't matter when it comes to resilience. The harpy eagle, with its formidable talons, is the avian equivalent of a bodybuilder, capable of snatching monkeys from trees with ease.

Intelligence in animals is a fascinating field, and some creatures demonstrate cognitive abilities that can rival our own. Octopuses, with their problem-solving prowess, have been known to escape enclosures, use tools, and even open jars to get to their dinner. They're like the Houdinis of the ocean, only with more arms and a penchant for seafood. Crows and ravens, those feathered Einsteins, use tools and have memories so sharp they can remember the faces of people who have wronged them. They're the Sherlocks of the bird world, solving puzzles that would leave lesser creatures scratching their heads. Dolphins, with their complex communication and teamwork, orchestrate hunting strategies that would make military generals green with envy. And elephants, with their intricate social structures and learning behaviors, demonstrate empathy, cooperation, and memory in ways that are both heartwarming and humbling.

Quirky animal records offer a delightful glimpse into the extraordinary. Take Jonathan the tortoise, who at over 188 years old, is the Methuselah of the animal kingdom. He's seen more birthdays than most of us will ever attend, and he's still going strong. Zeus, the Great Dane, stood at a towering 44 inches tall, making other dogs look like toys. Meanwhile, Milly the Chihuahua, at just 3.8 inches tall, could fit in your pocket—or your teacup—without any trouble. And then there's Waffle the Warrior Cat, who leaped an impressive 7 feet, proving that sometimes cats don't just land on their feet—they fly.

3.2 Extraordinary Achievements in Science and Technology

The realm of space exploration is a testament to human ingenuity and audacity, marked by achievements that were once the stuff of science fiction. When Neil Armstrong took that "giant leap for mankind" on July 20, 1969, the world held its breath. The Apollo 11 mission wasn't just about planting a flag or collecting moon rocks; it was about proving that humanity could transcend earthly bounds. Armstrong's footstep symbolized a new era, one where the sky was no longer the limit. Fast forward to the Voyager probes, launched in 1977 and still zipping around in the vastness of space in 2024. These plucky little spacecraft have traveled beyond the solar system, sending back postcards from the final frontier. Their journey reminds us that curiosity doesn't just kill cats—it propels us into the cosmos.

Closer to home, the Mars Rover missions, particularly Curiosity and Perseverance, have been our robotic eyes and ears on the Red Planet. These rovers, equipped with advanced scientific instruments, have been trundling across Martian terrain, uncovering secrets of a world that might have once harbored life. Their findings spark the imagination, fueling dreams of future Martian colonies and interplanetary travel. Meanwhile, floating above us, the Hubble Space Telescope has revolutionized our understanding of the universe. Since its launch in 1990, Hubble has gifted us with breathtaking images of galaxies, nebulae, and stars, expanding our cosmic horizons and reminding us of the beauty and vastness of the universe.

The rest of the story: The Hubble Space Telescope, launched in 1990, faced a significant challenge early on: its primary mirror was incorrectly shaped due to a miscalculation, causing images to blur. This design flaw, creating spherical aberration, threatened to undermine its mission. However, NASA didn't retreat. In 1993, the Space Shuttle Endeavour carried a crew on mission STS-61 to perform an unprecedented in-space repair. The solution involved installing the Corrective Optics Space Telescope Axial Replacement (COSTAR) system and a new camera, the Wide Field and Planetary Camera 2 (WFPC2), both designed to correct the flawed optics. Through a series of meticulously planned spacewalks, astronauts replaced the defective parts and installed new gyroscopes to stabilize the telescope. Post-repair, Hubble's images were transformed, showcasing the universe's splendor with unprecedented clarity. This mission not only restored Hubble's vision but also highlighted the incredible potential of human ingenuity in overcoming the vast challenges of space exploration. The successful correction of Hubble's mirror has since enabled it to capture breathtaking cosmic phenomena, significantly contributing to our understanding of the universe. It stands as a testament to the importance of precision engineering and the resilience of space missions, paving the way for future explorations and technological advancements in orbit.

In the world of medicine, few discoveries have had as profound an impact as penicillin. Discovered by Alexander Fleming in 1928, this accidental miracle changed the course of medicine, ushering in the age of antibiotics and saving countless lives. Before penicillin, even a minor cut could spell doom, but now, bacteria didn't stand a chance. Then there's Jonas Salk, the man who declared war on polio and won. His development of the polio vaccine not only eradicated a crippling disease but also inspired a generation of scientists to pursue vaccines for other scourges. The Human Genome Project, completed in 2003, mapped the entire human genome, opening up a new frontier in biology. Suddenly, the blueprint of life was at our fingertips, promising advances in personalized medicine and genetic therapy. And let's not overlook the first successful organ transplant, a breakthrough that transformed medical possibilities and gave new hope to patients worldwide. More recently, the Neuralink brain implant chip aims to help quadriplegics communicate and interact with the world by translating thoughts into digital signals, bridging the gap between mind and machine.

Technological innovation has been the backbone of modern society, reshaping how we live, work, and play. Remember the days of dial-up modems and bulletin boards? If you ever waited for a web page to load while your computer screeched like a robotic banshee, you know that patience was indeed a virtue. These early digital pioneers paved the way for the internet, a marvel conceived by visionaries like Vint Cerf and Tim Berners-Lee. This "information superhighway" has changed everything, from how we shop to how we date. Then came the smartphone, a device that put the world in our pockets and made communication as easy as a swipe or a tap. Today, we can't imagine life without our tiny digital companions, even if they do occasionally autocorrect "love" to "lava."

3.3 The rest of the story: Modems.

The Evolution of Data Transfer: From Dial-Up to Terabit Speeds

1960s–1970s: 300 Baud Modem - Speed: 0.3 kbps - Highlight: The dawn of home computing, enabling basic text communication.

1970s–1980s: 1200 Baud Modem - Speed: 1.2 kbps - Highlight: Improved speeds for downloading small files and early graphical images.

1980s: 2400 Baud Modem - Speed: 2.4 kbps - Highlight: Enhanced reliability for connecting to online services and bulletin board systems (BBSs).

Mid-1980s–1990s: 9600 Baud Modem - Speed: 9.6 kbps - Highlight: A leap forward, supporting early online services.

1990s: 14.4 Kbps Modem - Speed: 14.4 kbps - Highlight: Made early web browsing more feasible, despite simplistic website designs.

1990s: 28.8 & 33.6 Kbps Modems - Speed: 28.8/33.6 kbps - Highlight: Web browsing became more practical as multimedia content grew.

Late 1990s–Early 2000s: 56 Kbps Modem - Speed: 56 kbps - Highlight: Represented the pinnacle of dial-up speeds, but large files still loaded slowly.

Late 1990s–2000s: DSL & Cable Modems - Speed: 128 kbps to 1+ Mbps - Highlight: Marked the transition to broadband, offering always-on connections and transforming internet use.

2000s–Present: Fiber Optic Internet - Speed: 10 Mbps to 1 Gbps and beyond - Highlight: Utilizing light signals for data transfer, drastically improving internet speeds and capabilities.

2020s–Present: 5G Wireless Networks - Speed: Up to 10 Gbps - Highlight: Introduces high-speed internet to mobile, enabling advanced applications like augmented reality.

2020s–Present: Current Gigabit Connections - Speed: 1 Gbps to 10 Gbps - Highlight: Fiber-optic and advanced cable technologies make gigabit speeds widespread, supporting data-heavy applications.

Future: Terabit Speeds - Speed: 1 Tbps and beyond - Highlight: Research into 6G and next-gen fiber optics promises to unlock even faster, real-time data transfer across various sectors.

This concise history underscores the monumental leaps in technology that have exponentially increased the speed and reliability of our internet connections, paving the way for a future where data transfer knows virtually no bounds.

Advances in renewable energy technology signal a shift toward a more sustainable future. Solar panels and wind turbines have become symbols of (false) hope in the battle against climate change, harnessing the power of nature to fuel our lives. Meanwhile, artificial intelligence and machine learning algorithms are transforming industries, making everything from virtual assistants to self-driving cars possible. These technologies, once the realm of science fiction, are now integral to our daily routines, offering glimpses of a future where machines might do the laundry or even cook dinner.

Engineering marvels continue to astound us, pushing the boundaries of what is possible. Structures like the Burj Khalifa, the tallest building in the world, pierce the sky with audacious elegance, while the Millau Viaduct in France stretches across valleys like a concrete ribbon, marrying form and function. These feats of engineering aren't just about height or length; they're about vision, creativity, and the human spirit's relentless drive to reach new heights. The Panama Canal, a monumental project completed in 1914, redefined global trade routes, showcasing the ability to transform geographic barriers into pathways for progress. As we stand in awe of these achievements, we are reminded that while we may be small in the grand scheme of things, our aspirations and abilities are anything but.

4

Chapter 4: Geography

Imagine this: you're standing in the city of La Paz, Bolivia, trying not to gasp for breath. It's not because of the stunning views or the vibrant culture, but because you're in the highest capital city in the world, perched at a dizzying 3,869 meters or 12,693 feet above sea level. Just breathing here feels like an achievement worthy of a trophy. La Paz is one of those capitals that defies the ordinary, serving as a reminder that geography is as much about heights and depths as it is about politics and culture.

Speaking of capitals, did you know that South Africa couldn't settle for just one? It has three! Pretoria, Cape Town, and Bloemfontein each take turns playing capital, like siblings sharing a particularly prestigious toy. This tri-capital setup is a nod to the country's diverse history and the desire to spread government functions across its regions, ensuring no city feels left out of the fun.

And then there's Nauru, which decided that having a capital was too mainstream. As the second smallest country in the world, Nauru is content to function without a capital city, proving that sometimes less is more, especially when it comes to bureaucracy.

Now, let's pivot to some of the world's most famous landmarks, each with its own set of secrets and stories. The Eiffel Tower, for example, isn't just a pretty face. Gustave Eiffel, the tower's mastermind, built a secret apartment at the top. Imagine the view! It's the perfect spot for a little peace and quiet—unless you're afraid of heights. Today, visitors can peek inside and see wax figures of Eiffel and his guests, making you wonder if he ever hosted parties up there with the world's most exclusive guest list.

In the United States, Mount Rushmore isn't just about presidential faces. Behind Abraham Lincoln's majestic cranium lies a hidden Hall of Records. This secret chamber holds copies of important U.S. documents, like a governmental time capsule perched high on a mountain. It's as if the founding fathers foresaw the day when future generations would need a quiet place to ponder the mysteries of democracy, or perhaps just to escape the hustle and bustle of tourist season.

Meanwhile, the Great Wall of China stretches across the landscape like a colossal dragon, an impressive feat of engineering and endurance. While most of us would struggle to assemble a flat-pack bookshelf, ancient Chinese laborers pieced together this monumental structure brick by brick. It's a testament to human perseverance and perhaps a little overzealousness in keeping out nosy neighbors.

The Taj Mahal, India's ode to love and architectural wonder, also has its mysteries. Legend has it that Shah Jahan, the emperor who commissioned the monument, planned a black marble mausoleum for himself across the river. Unfortunately, his son had other ideas, imprisoning Shah Jahan before he could build the matching set. It's a reminder that even in the grandest of projects, family drama can ruin your plans faster than an uninvited relative at Thanksgiving.

Now, let's talk about the fascinating micro-nations dotting the globe like secret levels in a video game. Take Vatican City, for example, the world's smallest independent state, snugly nestled within Rome, Italy. Despite its size, it wields significant influence, proving that you don't need sprawling lands to make a big impact. Monaco, a small country within the borders of France, with its glamorous reputation and tax perks, is another pint-sized powerhouse. It's like the James Bond of countries—small, sleek, and always dressed to impress.

Liechtenstein is a charming little principality tucked between Switzerland and Austria. With a population smaller than most mid-sized towns, 39,870 as of 2024, it embraced the "less is more" philosophy long before it was trendy. These micro-nations remind us that sometimes the best things come in small packages—unless you're talking about chocolate, in which case, more is always better.

Borders, those invisible lines that separate one country from another, often have stories as interesting as the countries themselves. Take the curious case of Lesotho, a country entirely surrounded by South Africa. It's like a geographical nesting doll, a country within a country, maintaining its independence despite being enveloped on all sides. Then there's the Vatican, entirely encircled by the city of Rome, proving that Rome wasn't built in a day, but it sure can build around you.

On the other end of the spectrum, we have the longest border in the world: the one between Canada and the United States. Stretching over 8,800 kilometers, or 5,468 miles, it's a testament to the enduring friendship and occasional sibling rivalry between the two nations. It's so long that if you tried to walk it, you'd likely wear out several pairs of shoes.

For something a little more compact, consider the border between Spain and Gibraltar. At just 1.2 kilometers, 3/4 of a mile, it's the world's shortest international border. Blink and you might miss it, but it serves as a reminder that even the tiniest borders can hold enormous historical and political significance.

Geography isn't just about maps and coordinates; it's a story of cultures, histories, and the sometimes quirky boundaries that define our world.

4.1 Trivia about Geographical Oddities Providing a Global Perspective

Imagine a hill where cars seem to defy gravity, rolling uphill as if the laws of physics decided to take a day off. Welcome to the world of magnetic hills, where the landscape plays tricks on your mind and your GPS. Found in places like Ladakh in India and Moncton in Canada, these hills create the illusion that cars can coast uphill, powered by nothing more than an optical illusion. It's all thanks to the surrounding terrain, which tricks your eyes into seeing a slope where there isn't one. If you've ever wanted to feel like you're driving in a cartoon, these mysterious hills offer a chance to experience a gravity-defying ride, with no special effects required. See a list of locations around the world where these effects are seen in the next chapter.

But gravity isn't the only thing that acts strangely in the world of geographical oddities. Take disappearing lakes, for example. One moment, they're there, and the next, poof! Gone, like socks in a dryer. In places like Oregon's Lost Lake, the water vanishes through volcanic tubes, leaving behind a dry bed that looks like nature's idea of a practical joke. During the rainy season, the lake fills up, only to drain away again like a giant bathtub. It's a natural marvel that keeps locals guessing and tourists scratching their heads, wondering if they should have packed their swimsuits or a Frisbee.

Speaking of water, the Earth's oceans hold secrets so deep they make the Mariana Trench—the planet's deepest oceanic point—an enigma. At nearly 11,000 meters, about 36,000 feet, this trench is more than just a deep hole; it's an abyss that challenges explorers and sparks the imagination. The pressure at the bottom is so intense that it could crush a submarine like a soda can, yet life thrives in its dark depths. Strange creatures with bioluminescent features call this place home, evolving to survive in an environment more alien than the surface of the moon. It's a reminder that no matter how much we think we know, the ocean always has a few tricks up its sleeve.

...crush... like a soda can...### The Evolution of Soda Cans: A Journey Through Time The story of soda cans mirrors the march of innovation, reflecting our changing needs and technological advances. Initially, soda cans were bulky, steel containers that made their debut in the early 20th century. These cans were cumbersome and required a tool to open, making them less user-friendly but valued for their durability in military rations and food storage. The 1950s marked a turning point with the introduction of aluminum, a lighter and corrosion-resistant material that revolutionized the soda can industry. This shift not only made cans more portable but also streamlined production and distribution, paving the way for the beverage can we recognize today. Innovation didn't stop at materials. The "cone-top" can, a precursor to the modern design, featured a bottle-like shape and needed a key for opening. However, the real breakthrough came in 1962 with Ermal Fraze's invention of the pop-top can, introducing a ring pull mechanism that eliminated the need for additional tools. The 1970s saw the advent of the pull-tab, a fully removable version that, while popular, raised environmental concerns due to littering. Responding to these concerns, the stay-on-tab was developed by the Reynolds Metals Company in 1975. This design improvement ensured the tab remained attached to the can after opening, enhancing safety and reducing litter. Today's soda cans embody over six decades of innovation: they are lightweight, made from recyclable aluminum, and feature the universally adopted stay-on-tab mechanism. Standard cans typically hold 12 oz (355 mL) of liquid, but sizes can vary, offering choices from the compact 7.5 oz to larger 16 oz or 24 oz options. From the early steel versions to today's sleek aluminum cans, these containers have evolved to become a convenient, environmentally friendly solution for beverage packaging.

In the late 1960s, my brother showed me the structural strength of a cylinder by balancing his entire weight on a soda can. He also showed me how to crush those earlier thicker aluminum soda cans by creasing four sides of the can with opposing thumbs and once the cylinder walls were disrupted, the can could be crushed.

From the depths of the ocean to the heights of the Earth, Mount Everest stands as the tallest mountain above sea level, a giant that looms over the Himalayan range. But did you know it's not the closest point to space on Earth? That honor belongs to Mount Chimborazo in Ecuador, thanks to the Earth's equatorial bulge. While Everest may be the highest peak, Chimborazo's summit is the farthest from the Earth's core, making it the ultimate perch for those aiming to be just a little closer to the stars. It's a geographical quirk that would make any trivia enthusiast's heart soar, a testament to how our planet's shape influences everything from gravity to geography.

Now let's transition from lofty heights to remote islands, where the world feels both vast and intimate at the same time. Take Tristan da Cunha, for instance, the most isolated inhabited island in the world, located smack in the middle of the South Atlantic Ocean. Living here means having neighbors who are a seven-day boat ride away, making it the perfect spot for those who truly want to "get away from it all." This tiny speck of land is home to just a few hundred residents, a close-knit community that thrives despite its remoteness. It's an island where time seems to stand still, offering a glimpse into a way of life that's as rare as a solar eclipse.

But not all islands are inhabited. Consider the mystery of North Sentinel Island, part of the Andaman and Nicobar archipelago in the Indian Ocean. This island is home to the Sentinelese, a tribe that remains untouched by modern civilization, living in voluntary isolation. They fiercely protect their island from outsiders, making it one of the most enigmatic and uncontacted places on Earth. It's a testament to the diversity of human existence, reminding us that even in our connected world, some places remain shrouded in mystery and tradition. As you ponder these islands, you might wonder about the secrets they hold, the stories untold, and the cultures untainted by time.

Another island worth mentioning is Socotra, an archipelago off the coast of Yemen that looks like it was plucked straight from a science fiction novel. Its unique ecosystem is home to the Dragon's Blood Tree, a bizarre umbrella-shaped plant that oozes red sap. Socotra's flora and fauna evolved in isolation, creating a landscape that's both alien and awe-inspiring. It's like stepping into a world where evolution took a sharp left turn, leaving behind wonders that defy imagination. This island is a reminder that our planet is a tapestry of biodiversity, each thread more intricate and colorful than the last.

As we wrap up our exploration of geographical oddities, it's clear that our planet is a treasure trove of wonders, from the whimsical to the mind-boggling. These natural features remind us that while we may map and measure the world, it still holds secrets and surprises that can leave us in awe. Whether it's a hill that laughs in the face of gravity, a lake with a disappearing act, or an island that feels like another world, these oddities challenge our understanding and ignite our curiosity. As we move forward, let's keep our sense of wonder alive, ready to uncover the next geographical marvel that awaits just beyond the horizon.

5

Chapter 5: Nature's Mysteries

Picture this: you're swimming in the ocean, minding your own business, when suddenly the water around you starts to glow like a scene straight out of a sci-fi movie. No, you're not in a remake of "The Abyss." You've just encountered the magical phenomenon of bioluminescence. This natural light show is brought to you by Mother Nature's very own disco ball—bioluminescent creatures. But don't worry, there are no cover charges or bouncers here, just a dazzling display of nature's brilliance.

Bioluminescence is the process by which living organisms produce light. Imagine a tiny chemical laboratory inside a creature, where luciferin and luciferase get together for a little chemical reaction party. When these two molecules meet oxygen, they produce light. It's like a glow stick, but far more sophisticated and without the risk of accidentally cracking it open and getting that neon liquid everywhere. Unlike fluorescence, which requires external light to shine, bioluminescence generates its own light, making it the ultimate energy-efficient nightlight.

Enter the marine realm, where bioluminescence reigns supreme. Deep-sea anglerfish are the rock stars of this underwater world, using their bioluminescent lures to attract prey. It's like a fish version of a moth to a flame, except the moth is dinner and the flame is a glowing appendage dangling in the dark. Then there's the glowing jellyfish, which drift through the ocean's depths like ethereal chandeliers, lighting up the water with their gentle, pulsating glow. These creatures have mastered the art of living in the abyss, turning darkness into a canvas for their luminous displays. And let's not forget about the dinoflagellates, the microscopic plankton responsible for the "milky seas" phenomenon. When disturbed, these tiny organisms emit a bluish glow, creating an otherworldly effect that has left sailors and night swimmers in awe for centuries.

But bioluminescence isn't limited to the ocean. On land, fireflies put on summer evening performances that rival any fireworks display. These little beetles use their flashing lights to communicate, find mates, and perhaps even engage in a little firefly flirting. It's the ultimate light show, complete with an unspoken promise of romance in the night air. Meanwhile, in the forests of North America, bioluminescent fungi like the "foxfire" fungus glow eerily in the dark, casting an ethereal light on the forest floor. And let's not overlook the glowing millipedes of

California, which shine with a soft green glow to ward off predators. It's nature's way of saying, "I'm toxic, but aren't I pretty?"

The practical applications of bioluminescence are as fascinating as the creatures themselves. In medical research, scientists use bioluminescent markers to track cells and pathogens, illuminating the inner workings of biological processes in a way that's both enlightening and awe-inspiring. Environmentalists use bioluminescence to detect pollution, allowing them to monitor the health of ecosystems with a glow-in-the-dark flair. And, of course, artists and entertainers have embraced bioluminescence, creating glow-in-the-dark products that add a touch of whimsy to our lives. From glow sticks at concerts to luminous art installations, bioluminescence has found a place in our culture, lighting up our world in ways that are as beautiful as they are unexpected.

Bioluminescence is a reminder that nature is the ultimate artist, painting the world with light in the most unexpected places. Whether deep in the ocean or in your backyard, these glowing wonders invite us to marvel at the mysteries of the natural world.

Before we leave the mysteries of the sea, consider this, the heart of a shrimp is located in its head, a unique characteristic compared to many other animals. Specifically, the heart is situated behind the eyes, within the thoracic region, which is part of the head structure in shrimp. This placement allows for efficient circulation within their open circulatory system, where the heart pumps a fluid called hemolymph, rather than blood, throughout the body. The hemolymph flows freely around the organs, delivering oxygen and nutrients without a closed network of blood vessels. The internal anatomy of shrimp and other crustaceans is quite different from that of mammals, with many organs located in the head region.

5.1 Mystical Forests and Their Secrets

Forests have long been the world's most enigmatic gathering places, where the rustle of leaves could just as easily be a breeze or the whisper of ancient spirits. Take the Black Forest in Germany, a place so steeped in folklore that even the trees seem to have stories to tell. This dense woodland is the birthplace of fairy tales, where Hansel and Gretel might have wandered, leaving a trail of breadcrumbs behind. Legend has it that the forest is home to dwarfs, witches, and even the mischievous Kobold, a spirit known for playing pranks on unsuspecting travelers. It's as if the forest itself is a living, breathing character in a Grimm Brothers' tale, shrouded in mystery and a touch of magic.

Across the globe, Japan's Aokigahara, also known as the "Sea of Trees," presents a stark contrast. This forest is as quiet as a library on a Monday morning, with an eerie stillness that seems to swallow sound. Nestled at the base of Mount Fuji, Aokigahara is infamous for its reputation as a place where many have gone to end their lives, giving rise to ghost stories and tales of wandering spirits. Yet, it is also a place of immense beauty, where thick foliage and twisted trees create a natural labyrinth, offering solace and reflection for those who dare to enter.

Meanwhile, in the Khasi hills of India, sacred groves stand as a testament to a long-standing relationship between nature and spirituality. These groves have been preserved for centuries by local tribes who believe that the spirits of their ancestors reside within them. It's a place where nature and the divine intertwine, where the air is thick with the scent of moss and reverence. Here, every tree, rock, and stream holds a sacred significance, reminding us of the deep-rooted connection between humans and the natural world.

From mystical tales to biodiversity hotspots, forests are also the lungs of our planet, teeming with life and diversity. The Amazon Rainforest, often dubbed the "lungs of the Earth," is a vast expanse of greenery that supports an unparalleled array of species. From the majestic jaguar to the elusive pink river dolphin, this vibrant ecosystem is a testament to nature's ability to weave complexity and beauty into an intricate tapestry of life.

Madagascar's rainforests offer another glimpse into nature's creativity, home to species found nowhere else on Earth. Lemurs leap through the canopy, while chameleons change color as if auditioning for a nature documentary. It's a place where evolution has taken the scenic route, resulting in a menagerie of unique creatures that defy explanation.

Then there are the cloud forests, or rainforests of Central America, where mist hangs heavy in the air, creating an ethereal atmosphere that feels almost otherworldly. These forests are rich in biodiversity, harboring an array of plants and animals that thrive in the cool, moist environment. It's a place where you might encounter the resplendent quetzal, a bird so vibrant it looks like it flew straight out of a painting.

But not all forest mysteries are friendly. In Maryland's Black Hills Forest, the legends of the Blair Witch have sent shivers down the spines of even the bravest adventurers. The tales of disappearances and supernatural occurrences are enough to make you reconsider that late-night hike. Meanwhile, the Hoya-Baciu Forest in Romania has earned the nickname "Bermuda Triangle of Transylvania" due to the inexplicable vanishing of people who venture too far into its depths. And let's not forget the mysterious lights of North Carolina's Brown Mountain, where glowing orbs have been reported dancing along the ridge, defying scientific explanation and igniting the imagination.

In the face of such mysteries, efforts to conserve and protect these forests are more important than ever. Reforestation initiatives in the Amazon aim to restore the balance between human development and nature's splendor. In Madagascar, community-led conservation projects work tirelessly to safeguard the unique species that call this island home. International agreements and treaties strive to protect these ancient and mystical forests, ensuring that they remain sanctuaries for both nature and the human spirit.

5.2 Puzzling Geological Formations

Imagine standing at the edge of the Giant's Causeway in Northern Ireland, a geological wonder that looks like it was crafted by the world's most precise bricklayer. This natural marvel consists of about 40,000 interlocking basalt columns, formed by an ancient volcanic eruption. Legend has it that the causeway was built by the Irish giant Finn McCool as a bridge to Scotland, although geologists with their fancy degrees insist it was volcanic activity. Whether you believe in giants or geology, it's a sight that defies the ordinary, leaving visitors to ponder the mysteries of nature and ancient folklore.

In Arizona's Paria Canyon-Vermilion Cliffs, you'll find The Wave, a rock formation so surreal it feels like stepping into a painting by Salvador Dalí. Its swirling patterns and undulating lines are the result of millions of years of erosion, shaping the Navajo sandstone into a mesmerizing natural sculpture. Getting there requires a hike, a permit, and a sense of adventure, as only a limited number of people are allowed to visit each day. But those who make the trek are rewarded with a visual feast that challenges the boundaries of reality.

Meanwhile, on the other side of the globe, New Zealand offers the Moeraki Boulders, a series of large, spherical stones scattered along Koekohe Beach. These giant marbles are believed to have formed millions of years ago, emerging from the cliffs as waves erode the land. Some locals say they are the remnants of eel baskets washed ashore from a wrecked canoe, while scientists explain them as calcite concretions formed in ancient sea floor sediments. Whether you see them as ancient artifacts or just really big rocks, they add a mystical touch to the New Zealand coastline.

Also in New Zealand is Waitomo Caves which offers a different kind of subterranean magic. Here, glowworms light up the darkness, creating a starry sky underground. These tiny bioluminescent creatures dangle from the cave ceiling, casting an ethereal glow that guides visitors through the labyrinthine passages. It's a spectacle that feels like a natural planetarium, where the stars are just an arm's length away—though catching them might be frowned upon.

The world beneath our feet holds just as many mysteries as the skies above. In Mexico's Cave of Crystals, you'll find selenite crystals so massive they could make Superman's Fortress of Solitude look like a starter home. Discovered deep underground in the Naica Mine, these crystals are over 500,000 years old, formed by mineral-rich waters heated by magma. The conditions in the cave are so harsh, with temperatures reaching 58°C (136°F), that even the most adventurous explorers can only endure short visits. It's a hidden marvel, a testament to the secretive beauty of the Earth's interior.

In Vietnam, Son Doong Cave boasts the largest cave passage in the world, a cavern so vast it has its own weather system. Discovered only in the 1990s, this underground wonder features towering stalagmites, underground rivers, and even a jungle. Exploring Son Doong is like entering another world, a subterranean kingdom that challenges our understanding of what lies beneath the Earth's surface.

Back above ground, Death Valley's Racetrack Playa presents an unsolved mystery: rocks that move on their own. These "sailing stones" leave long trails in the dry lake bed, yet no one has ever seen them move. Recent studies suggest that a combination of ice sheets, wind, and just the right amount of water allows the rocks to slide across the playa, but the phenomenon remains a captivating enigma, inspiring tales of alien intervention and secret forces.

Crossing the Pacific, the Chocolate Hills of the Philippines presents another puzzle. These conical hills, numbering in the thousands, turn brown in the dry season, hence their name. Their formation remains a topic of debate, with theories ranging from coral deposits to volcanic activity. As you stand among these geological cupcakes, it's hard not to wonder about their true origins and the forces that shaped them.

In Western Australia, the Pinnacles Desert is a landscape dotted with limestone pillars rising from the sand, resembling a forest of stone sentinels. Formed millions of years ago from seashells, these eerie formations create a surreal scene straight out of a sci-fi movie. Walking among the Pinnacles, you might feel like an intergalactic explorer discovering a new planet, half-expecting a Martian to pop out from behind a pillar.

And then there's the Bermuda Triangle, a region infamous for its mysterious disappearances of ships and aircraft. While skeptics attribute these incidents to natural causes like rogue waves and methane hydrates, the Triangle's reputation as a supernatural hotspot persists, fueling imaginations and conspiracy theories alike.

In Turkmenistan, the "Door to Hell" offers a fiery spectacle—a gas crater that's been burning for decades after a drilling accident. This flaming pit draws curious travelers from around the world, a reminder of humanity's occasional blunders in the face of nature's might.

Finally, the magnetic hill phenomenon challenges our senses, as cars seemingly roll uphill against gravity. Found in various locations worldwide, these hills are optical illusions, where the surrounding landscape tricks our eyes and minds. It's a fun quirk of nature, a reminder that sometimes things aren't as they seem.

Here is a list of notable locations around the world where the **magnetic hill phenomenon** occurs

- Ladakh, India - Magnetic Hill near Leh
- Gansu Province, China - The "Magnetic Hill" in Lanzhou
- Namsan Park, South Korea
- Maharashtra, India - Tulsishyam Hill in the Gir Forest
- Moncton, Canada - Magnetic Hill in New Brunswick
- Los Angeles, California, USA - Mystery Spot in Griffith Park
- Pennsylvania, USA - Gravity Hill in Bedford County
- Salt Lake City, Utah, USA - Gravity Hill
- New Jersey, USA - Gravity Hill in Franklin Township
- Scotland, UK - Electric Brae in Ayrshire
- Romagna, Italy - Gravity Hill near Cesena
- Portugal - Gravity Hill in Braga
- Poland - Magnetic Hill in Karpacz
- Black Mountain, Queensland
- Orroroo, South Australia - Gravity Hill
- South Africa - Magnetic Hill near Harrismith, Free State Province
- Al Ain, UAE - Gravity Hill in the Jebel Hafeet area

As we leave these geological wonders behind, remember that the Earth's mysteries are as endless as they are fascinating.

Geology is the study of the Earth's physical structure, materials, and processes. It focuses on understanding the composition of the Earth's crust, the processes that have shaped the planet over time (such as plate tectonics, volcanic activity, and erosion), and how these processes have created the landforms and resources we see today. Geologists investigate the history of the Earth, including the origin of rocks, minerals, and fossils, and how they have evolved over millions of years. They also study natural hazards like earthquakes and volcanoes.

Geography, on the other hand, is the study of the Earth's surface, environments, and the relationships between humans and their environment. It is broader and more interdisciplinary than geology, combining elements of both the physical and social sciences. Geographers examine spatial patterns, climate, ecosystems, population distribution, and the impact of human activity on the environment. Geography can be divided into two main branches: physical geography (which overlaps with geology in studying landforms and climate) and human geography (which studies human cultures, societies, and the effects of human activity on landscapes).

In short, geology is concerned with the Earth's internal structure and history, while geography is more focused on the Earth's surface and the spatial relationships between natural and human-made phenomena.

5.3 Time-out: Here's a list of more than 40 unbelievable facts

1. Bananas are berries, but strawberries are not.
2. Honey never spoils. Archaeologists have found pots of honey in ancient Egyptian tombs that are over 3,000 years old and still perfectly edible.
3. A day on Venus is longer than a year on Venus. It takes Venus 243 Earth days to complete one rotation, but only 225 Earth days to orbit the Sun.
4. Venus's surface is hot enough to melt lead.
5. Sharks existed before trees. Sharks have been around for about 400 million years, while trees appeared around 350 million years ago.
6. Octopuses have three hearts. Two pump blood to the gills, while the third pumps it to the rest of the body.
7. There are more stars in the universe than grains of sand on all the Earth's beaches, but there are more trees on Earth than stars in the Milky Way galaxy.
8. Cows have best friends and can get stressed when separated from them.
9. Some turtles can breathe through their butts.
10. The shortest war in history was between Britain and Zanzibar on August 27, 1896. Zanzibar surrendered after 38 minutes. See more details in Chapter 10.2.
11. The Eiffel Tower can grow taller during the summer. Due to the expansion of iron, it can grow by up to 6 inches.
12. A single cloud can weigh more than 1 million pounds.
13. Rats can laugh when tickled.

14. In space, astronauts' height can increase by up to 2 inches due to spinal stretching.
15. Sloths can hold their breath longer than dolphins. They can hold their breath for up to 40 minutes underwater.
16. The shortest commercial flight in the world lasts just 57 seconds. It's between two islands in the Orkney Islands, Scotland.
17. A group of flamingos is called a "flamboyance."
18. There's a planet made of diamond. 55 Cancri e is a super-Earth exoplanet that might be largely made of carbon and diamond.
19. The longest hiccuping spree lasted 68 years.
20. Giraffes have no vocal cords.
21. Wombat poop is cube-shaped.
22. Koalas sleep up to 22 hours a day.
23. In Japan, there's a museum dedicated to rocks that look like faces.
24. A day on Earth is not exactly 24 hours. It's actually 23 hours, 56 minutes, and 4 seconds.
25. But a day on Earth is getting longer. The Earth's rotation is gradually slowing down, adding about 1.7 milliseconds to the day every century.
26. Water can boil and freeze at the same time. This phenomenon is called the "triple point.
27. The human nose can detect over 1 trillion different scents.
28. The longest wedding veil was longer than 63 football fields.
29. In ancient Rome, urine was used as a mouthwash.
30. Cats can't taste sweet things.

31. The Mona Lisa has no eyebrows. It was the fashion in Renaissance Florence to shave them off.
32. You can't hum while holding your nose.
33. A day on Saturn is only about 10.7 hours long.
34. Humans share 60% of their DNA with bananas.
35. The human body contains around 37.2 trillion cells.
36. The world's largest snowflake on record was 15 inches wide.
37. The Amazon Rainforest produces 20% of the world's oxygen.
38. A pineapple is not a single fruit, but a collection of many smaller fruits fused together.
39. A comet's tail always points away from the Sun, no matter its direction.
40. The first computer virus was created in 1983.
41. The longest-living animal in the world is the ocean quahog clam, which can live for over 500 years.
42. In 2006, Pluto was reclassified as a "dwarf planet."
43. Giant pandas spend up to 12 hours a day eating bamboo.

These facts highlight the incredible diversity and strange phenomena in our world and beyond!

6

Chapter 6: Laws and Customs You Won't Believe

Imagine a world where the most pressing legal question is whether or not you're allowed to wash your car on a Sunday. Welcome to Switzerland, where the sound of a hose spraying water on a day of rest is akin to a rock concert in a library. It's illegal to wash your car on Sundays because, apparently, the Swiss believe that even vehicles deserve a day off. Perhaps they fear that the sight of soap suds cascading down a windshield might offend the sensibilities of those enjoying a leisurely stroll. Either way, it's a law that makes you wonder if the Swiss are secretly in cahoots with the car wash industry. And don't forget about the Swiss law regarding guinea pigs from an earlier chapter.

Travel across the English Channel to the UK, and you'll find yourself pondering the legal ramifications of handling a salmon in suspicious circumstances. Yes, you read that right. Under the Salmon Act of 1986, it's illegal to handle this fishy delicacy in a way that might raise eyebrows. What exactly qualifies as "suspicious" remains a mystery, but one can only imagine the courtroom drama as a defense lawyer tries to argue that their client was merely giving the salmon a friendly handshake. It's a reminder that sometimes, the law is as slippery as the fish it's trying to protect.

Meanwhile, in Massachusetts, you might want to double-check your carpool arrangements. It's unlawful to drive with a gorilla in the backseat, a law that raises more questions than it answers. Was there a time when gorillas were the preferred travel companions for New Englanders? Did someone have a particularly wild ride that necessitated this legislation? Whatever the reason, it's a law that leaves you chuckling and grateful that your commute is limited to human passengers.

Animal laws can be just as baffling, especially when they dictate how fish should live. In Reggio Emilia, Italy, it's illegal to keep goldfish in round bowls. Apparently, the circular confines are deemed cruel, as they distort the fish's view of the world, possibly leading to existential crises among finned pets. It's a bit like living in a funhouse mirror, and the Italians, in their wisdom, decided that goldfish deserve better. So, they banned round bowls, ensuring that every goldfish can enjoy a life of rectangular serenity.

If you ever find yourself attending a wedding or funeral in Australia, be sure to leave your kangaroo at home. It's illegal to disrupt these solemn occasions with a bouncing marsupial, which makes sense when you consider the chaos that could ensue. Imagine a kangaroo hopping down the aisle, scattering flowers and guests alike. It's a law that, while humorous, also highlights the unique challenges of living in a country where kangaroos are as common as pigeons.

Speaking of animals, Alaska has a law that seems tailor-made for the social media age: it's illegal to wake a sleeping bear for a photo. While it might sound like common sense, it turns out that some people need a reminder not to poke a snoozing grizzly for the sake of a selfie. It's a law that says, "Don't poke the bear," both literally and figuratively, because disturbing a slumbering giant is a surefire way to ruin your vacation.

When it comes to food and drink, the world is full of quirky regulations. In Singapore, chewing gum is banned unless you have a prescription. This law, designed to keep the city clean, means that gum chewers must resort to cloak-and-dagger tactics just to enjoy a stick of Juicy Fruit. I asked an acquaintance if she ever chewed gum while growing up in Singapore, and she said "When I was a kid, I could only eat it at home, not in public." Meanwhile, in France, it's illegal to sell an E.T. doll because it lacks a human face. Apparently, the French take their toy regulations as seriously as their cheese, and anything that strays too far from the human form is deemed unacceptable.

Travel to Wisconsin, and you'll find a law that takes margarine-hatred to new heights. It's illegal to serve margarine as a substitute for butter in public places unless specifically requested. It seems that Wisconsinites, in their devotion to dairy, have declared that margarine is an imposter, a pretender to the buttery throne. It's a law that ensures every slice of toast in the state is accompanied by the real deal, much to the delight of butter aficionados everywhere.

Curious clothing laws add another layer of intrigue to the world of bizarre regulations. In the Maldives, it's illegal for tourists to wear bikinis except on private resort islands. This law is a nod to the country's cultural norms, reminding visitors to pack a sarong alongside their snorkel gear. Meanwhile, in Thailand, driving shirtless is a no-go. The law might be an attempt to prevent sunburn or perhaps just an effort to maintain some decorum on the road. Either way, it's a reminder that when in Thailand, it's best to keep your shirt on, especially if you're behind the wheel.

In Japan, the "Metabo Law" sets waistline limits, making it illegal to be overweight. This law aims to combat rising obesity rates, but the idea of legally mandated waist measurements sounds like something out of a dystopian novel. It's a law that encourages healthy living but also raises questions about personal freedom and the extent to which governments can regulate waistlines. With the most recent data from 2023, over 40% of adults in the United States are classified as obese, maybe it's a law worth considering, for health's sake.

6.1 Strange Festivities and Traditions

Imagine a festival where the primary objective is to hurl tomatoes at unsuspecting strangers. No, this isn't a cookout gone wrong; it's La Tomatina in Spain. Held annually in the town of Buñol, this festival sees participants engage in the world's most chaotic food fight, pelting each other with overripe tomatoes until the streets run red with tomato juice. It's a messy affair that leaves everyone looking like they've just escaped a particularly aggressive salsa-making class. Participants gleefully wade through a sea of squished tomatoes, their laughter mingling with the squelch of fruit underfoot. This event is a testament to the human spirit's ability to find joy in even the simplest—and silliest—of acts. In recent years, La Tomatina in Buñol, Spain, has used significant amounts of tomatoes during its famous food fight. In 2023, for instance, about 150,000 tomatoes were thrown, marking a continuation of the festival's scale This event, which typically attracts over 20,000 participants, involves a massive and colorful tomato battle that lasts for about an hour.

The tomatoes used for La Tomatina are grown specifically for the event in areas like Extremadura and Xilxes. These tomatoes are a special variety cultivated for their texture, which makes them ideal for the fight. Interestingly, these tomatoes aren't suitable for consumption but are produced just for the festival, ensuring that their cultivation and distribution contribute to the local economy.

Meanwhile, in England, the Cheese Rolling festival takes the concept of chasing after your dreams quite literally. Participants launch themselves down a steep hill in pursuit of a wheel of cheese, risking life and limb for the chance to claim the coveted dairy prize. The hill, Cooper's Hill in Gloucestershire, is so steep that most competitors end up tumbling head over heels, resembling a scene from an old slapstick comedy. It's a spectacle that draws crowds from all over, eager to witness brave souls throw caution—and their balance—to the wind in pursuit of glory and Gouda.

In a more tropical setting, Thailand hosts the Monkey Buffet Festival, a celebration that puts the focus on our primate cousins. Here, thousands of macaque monkeys are treated to a veritable feast of fruits, vegetables, and other treats, all laid out for their enjoyment. The event is not only a tourist attraction but also a gesture of appreciation for the monkeys, who are believed to bring good luck to the area. As the monkeys gorge themselves on the buffet, visitors are reminded of the whimsical relationship between humans and animals, where sometimes the line between host and guest is delightfully blurred.

Cultural rituals often carry deep significance, such as Japan's Setsubun, which involves the age-old practice of throwing beans to ward off evil spirits. As participants chant, "Oni wa soto, fuku wa uchi" (Demons out, luck in), they toss roasted soybeans out the door to ensure a prosperous year ahead. It's a charming tradition that combines superstition with a bit of fun, as families take part in this symbolic act of cleansing and renewal.

In Iceland, the Yule Lads make an appearance during the 13 days leading up to Christmas. These mischievous trolls, each with their own quirky personality, visit children and leave gifts in their shoes—or a rotten potato if they've been naughty. It's a festive tradition that adds a touch of whimsy to the holiday season, as children eagerly await the arrival of these playful pranksters. Meanwhile, in Bolivia, the Tinku festival involves ritualistic fighting, where participants engage in controlled combat to ensure a bountiful harvest. Though it may sound intense, this practice is steeped in tradition and serves as a symbolic release of tension, uniting communities in a shared hope for prosperity.

Bizarre seasonal celebrations take the form of Krampusnacht in Austria, where the fearsome figure of Krampus roams the streets, scaring children and adults alike. Dressed in devilish costumes, people participate in parades and parties, embracing the playful fright that this folklore figure brings. It's a night where the line between fear and festivity is blurred, reminding everyone that sometimes a good scare is just what the holiday spirit ordered.

In Mexico, the Day of the Dead transforms the country into a vibrant tapestry of color and emotion, as families honor their deceased loved ones with altars, marigolds, and sugar skulls. This celebration of life and death is a poignant reminder of the cyclical nature of existence, where memories are cherished and spirits are invited to partake in the festivities. In Finland, the tradition of "Eukonkanto," or wife-carrying, sees couples racing through obstacle courses, with husbands carrying their wives on their backs. The reward? The wife's weight in beer, of course. It's a lighthearted event that combines athleticism with humor, as participants navigate through muddy paths in pursuit of hops and glory.

Festivals that celebrate the absurd include the World Bog Snorkeling Championship in Wales, where competitors don snorkels and flippers to navigate a water-filled trench cut through a peat bog. It's a muddy, murky affair that challenges both endurance and sanity, as participants splash their way through the course, cheered on by spectators reveling in the delightful absurdity of it all. Meanwhile, in Finland, the Air Guitar World Championships invite contestants to strut their stuff with imaginary guitars, channeling their inner rock stars in a performance that's as much about passion as it is about pantomime. The lack of actual instruments doesn't deter these air guitarists, who pour their hearts into every riff and solo, proving that sometimes the best music is the kind you can't hear.

Spain's Baby Jumping Festival, or El Colacho, features men dressed as devils leaping over rows of infants laid out on mattresses. This peculiar tradition, believed to cleanse the babies of sin and ensure their protection from evil spirits, is a sight to behold. As the "devils" soar over the little ones, the air is filled with a mix of anticipation and relief, as the crowd witnesses this unusual rite of passage.

In these festivities and traditions, we find a world rich with color, humor, and a touch of madness. The human spirit's penchant for celebration, even in the most unconventional forms, speaks to our collective desire to connect, laugh, and embrace the peculiarities that make life so wonderfully unpredictable. As we turn the page, let's carry this spirit of whimsy with us, ready to explore the next chapter of our journey.

6.2 Time-out for a Trivia matching quiz #2

Words With Bizarre Meanings: Can you match these words to their meanings below?

A- **Bamboozled**

B- **Canoodle**

C- **Codswallop**

D- **Dingleberry**

E- **Discombobulated**

F- **Flabbergasted**

G- **Flibbertigibbet**

H- **Kerfuffle**

I- **Malarky**

J- **Nincompoop**

K- **Persnickety**

L- **Poppycock**

M- **Pumpernickel**

N- **Shenanigans**

O- **Skedaddle**

P- **Thingamajig**

Q- **Whatchamacallit**

R- **Whippersnapper**

1. A commotion, fuss, or disturbance, usually caused by a disagreement or confusion
2. A foolish or silly person
3. A frivolous, talkative, or flighty person who is often seen as silly or gossipy

4. A placeholder term used when the actual name of an object is forgotten or unknown
5. A type of dark, dense rye bread, originally from Germany
6. A young, inexperienced person who is perceived as overconfident or presumptuous
7. Another placeholder term similar to "thingamajig," is used for an item whose name one cannot recall
8. Confused, disoriented, or unsettled
9. Extremely surprised or shocked; astonished
10. Mischievous or playful activities, often involving trickery or pranks
11. Nonsense or foolish talk; something that is silly or not true
12. Nonsense or something that is absurd and untrue
13. Overly fussy, picky, or concerned with trivial details
14. Silly talk, nonsense, or something that is insincere or exaggerated
15. This can refer to either a small, annoying piece of dried fecal matter caught in hair or, informally, a foolish or inept person
16. To be deceived, tricked, or confused by someone, often in a playful or sneaky manner
17. To engage in affectionate behavior like cuddling, hugging, or kissing
18. To leave quickly or run away in a hurry

Trivia matching quiz answers

1-H, 2-J, 3-G, 4-P, 5-M, 6-R, 7-Q, 8-E, 9-F, 10-N, 11-C, 12-L, 13-K, 14-I, 15-D, 16-A, 17-B, 18-O

Trivia matching quiz chart in Chapter 13.1

7

Chapter 7: Time Travel and Sci-Fi Wonders

Imagine yourself sipping on your morning coffee when, suddenly, a future version of you walks in, looks at your choice of outfit, and shakes their head disapprovingly. Before you can ask what went wrong in the wardrobe department, they vanish, leaving you with more questions than answers. Welcome to the baffling world of time travel, where the past, present, and future are as intertwined as your headphones after five minutes in your pocket. The concept has intrigued scientists and storytellers alike, from Einstein's relativity theories to the countless movies where paradoxes are treated as minor inconveniences rather than potential universe-destroying events.

7.1 Theories of Time Travel in Science

When Albert Einstein wasn't busy revolutionizing physics with his wild hair and snappy bow ties, he was laying the groundwork for time travel theories with his general theory of relativity.

According to Einstein, time is not a rigid, unchanging entity but more like a rubber band that can stretch and warp, especially near massive objects like black holes. This leads us to the concept of time dilation, where time moves slower the faster you go or the stronger the gravitational pull you experience. So, theoretically, if you could zip around the universe at the speed of light, you'd age more slowly than your earthbound pals—though you might miss a few birthdays along the way. And while you're pondering that, consider wormholes: those cosmic shortcuts through space and time that could, in theory, allow you to pop in and out of different eras like a temporal tourist. The catch? We have yet to find these interstellar highways, and even if we did, keeping them stable might require exotic matter with negative mass, which sounds as fictional as a unicorn on roller skates.

But if wormholes don't tickle your sci-fi fancy, perhaps quantum mechanics will. Enter the realm of quantum entanglement, where particles separated by vast distances can remain interconnected, behaving as if they're in a long-distance relationship that laughs in the face of traditional physics. This spooky action at a distance, as Einstein called it, raises questions about the very nature of time and space. Then there's quantum tunneling, where particles pass through barriers in ways that make you question if they've read the rulebook on physics. Imagine a world where these principles allow for time travel, with timelines branching out into parallel universes like a tree of infinite possibilities. It's a tantalizing thought—unless, of course, you end up in a universe where socks always disappear in the laundry.

For those who prefer their time travel theories with a side of cosmic grandeur, cosmic strings might be just the ticket. These hypothetical one-dimensional loops, thinner than an atom but heavier than the sun, could warp space-time in such a way that closed timelike curves (CTCs) become possible. Picture a loop in time where you can return to your starting point, like taking a stroll through a temporal garden path. Science fiction has had a field day with these concepts, envisioning time loops where characters relive the same day until they learn the error of their ways—or just get really good at karaoke. But these loops aren't just for narrative convenience; they raise genuine scientific inquiries about the nature of time itself.

Of course, no discussion of time travel would be complete without acknowledging the practical challenges and paradoxes that come with it. The grandfather paradox, for instance, poses a classic conundrum: if you travel back in time and accidentally prevent your grandparents from meeting, how do you exist to take that trip in the first place? It's the kind of existential puzzle that keeps philosophers and screenwriters up at night. Meanwhile, the bootstrap paradox asks how an object or piece of information can exist without ever being created, like a book that inspires its own author. These paradoxes might seem like a headache for future time travelers, but some clever minds have proposed solutions, such as the Novikov self-consistency principle, which suggests that actions taken by a time traveler are part of history all along, ensuring that paradoxes cannot occur.

In the end, while the theories and mathematics behind time travel might seem like a cosmic joke without a punchline, they offer a tantalizing glimpse into what could be possible, should the universe ever decide to grant us a backstage pass to its temporal tapestry.

7.2 Sci-Fi Technologies That Became Reality

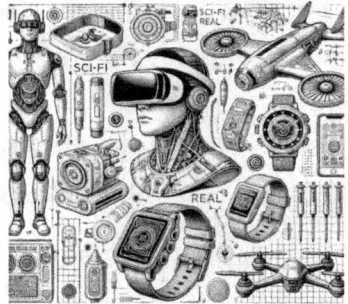

Picture this: you're in the 1960s, watching "Star Trek," and Captain Kirk casually whips out his communicator to chat with the crew. Fast forward a few decades, and here we are, pulling out our phones to order pizza like it's no big deal. The transformation from sci-fi fantasy to everyday reality is nothing short of astonishing. Inspired by those iconic "Star Trek" communicators, Martin Cooper and his team at Motorola developed the first mobile phone in 1973. It was an unwieldy brick that could make calls and develop biceps, but it paved the way for the sleek smartphones we can't live without today. Now, these devices do everything from tracking our steps to helping us win arguments with a quick Google search, all while fitting snugly in our pockets. They've evolved from clunky gadgets to indispensable lifelines, proving that sometimes, reality can outshine fiction.

Speaking of outshining fiction, let's talk about 3D printing—a technology that would make any "Star Trek" fan's heart skip a beat. In the series, replicators could whip up anything from a cup of Earl Grey tea to a violin. While we're not quite there yet, 3D printing has come a long way since its inception in the 1980s. It started with simple plastic models, but now, it's being used to print everything from human organs to rocket engine parts. In medicine, 3D printers create custom prosthetics and even human tissue, offering a new lease on life for many. Meanwhile, in manufacturing, they allow for rapid prototyping and custom designs, revolutionizing production lines. And let's not forget food printing—yes, you can now print your own pizza, though it might not rival your favorite pizzeria just yet. The potential for 3D printing in space exploration is equally thrilling, with the ability to print tools and habitats on Mars, turning science fiction into tangible reality.

When it comes to artificial intelligence and robotics, Isaac Asimov's laws of robotics laid the groundwork for a world where humans and machines coexist. Today, AI systems like IBM's Watson showcase the power of machine learning, analyzing data faster than you can say "Jeopardy champion." From industrial robots on factory floors to humanoid robots like Sophia engaging in charming banter, the evolution of robotics is nothing short of remarkable. But as we edge closer to a future where robots could become our colleagues, ethical considerations come into play. Can we trust them with decisions? Will they develop a sense of humor, or will they forever be the masters of dad jokes? These are the questions we must ponder as we continue to push the boundaries of artificial intelligence.

And then there's virtual reality, a concept that once existed solely in the realm of "Star Trek: The Next Generation" with its iconic holodeck. Early VR systems were clunky and limited, more likely to make you dizzy than immerse you in another world. But today, modern VR headsets offer experiences that transport users into fully realized virtual environments. Whether you're exploring ancient ruins, training for space missions, or just slicing through fruit with ninja-like precision, VR has found applications in gaming, education, and therapy. It's not just about gaming; therapists use VR to help patients overcome phobias, while companies use it for immersive training programs. As technology continues to advance, the line between virtual and reality blurs further, opening up possibilities that are as exciting as they are unpredictable.

7.3 Iconic Sci-Fi Books and Their Predictions

George Orwell's "1984" is the kind of book that makes you want to throw your smartphone out the window and cover your webcam with duct tape. Orwell envisioned a future where Big Brother wasn't just a nosy sibling but an all-seeing government entity. The phrase "Big Brother is watching you" has become a cultural shorthand for mass surveillance, tapping into our modern anxieties about privacy and government overreach. It's hard not to draw parallels between Orwell's dystopian world and our current reality, where surveillance cameras appear to outnumber pigeons, and data collection seems to be a national pastime. Orwell's portrayal of propaganda and thought control resonates in today's era of fake news and social media manipulation, where the truth is often as elusive as a Wi-Fi signal in the wilderness. The book's relevance endures, serving as both a cautionary tale and a reflection of contemporary political regimes that seem to have misplaced the memo on personal freedoms.

Ray Bradbury's "Fahrenheit 451" brings the heat—literally and figuratively—with its depiction of a future where firemen don't douse flames but ignite them to burn books. The novel explores themes of censorship and the numbing effect of superficial entertainment, painting a world where critical thinking is as obsolete as VHS tapes. Bradbury's firemen torch literature to suppress dissenting ideas, a concept that echoes in today's discussions about censorship and information control, where controversial books face bans and social media platforms grapple with content moderation. The book also critiques the impact of television and passive consumption on society, a prophetic nod to our current binge-watching culture, where watching an entire series in one sitting is both a badge of honor and a cry for help. Amidst the blaze, Bradbury emphasizes the enduring importance of literature and critical thinking, reminding us that sometimes, it's the stories we tell that keep us human.

William Gibson's "Neuromancer" catapulted us into cyberspace before most of us had even heard of dial-up modems. Gibson envisioned a world where the lines between the physical and digital blur, introducing the concept of the Matrix long before Neo donned his iconic sunglasses. In this gritty cyberpunk landscape, hackers navigate virtual realms with a dexterity that would make today's IT wizards blush. The novel's portrayal of cyber warfare and digital subterfuge foreshadowed the rise of cybersecurity concerns and the internet's evolution into a vast, interconnected web of both opportunity and peril. Gibson's influence is palpable in the development of the internet and the cyberpunk culture that embraces the fusion of technology and humanity. His work predicted technological trends and societal shifts, painting a digital future that feels both familiar and futuristic, like a retro vision of tomorrow.

H.G. Wells' "The Time Machine" is the granddaddy of time travel tales, inviting readers to ponder the possibilities of moving through the fourth dimension. Wells' invention of the time machine itself became a cultural icon, inspiring countless stories where characters skip through time like stones across a pond. But this isn't just a tale of temporal joyrides; it's a social commentary on class divisions and the evolution of humanity. Wells' vision of a future where society splits into the decadent Eloi and the laboring Morlocks offers a biting critique of class disparity, a theme that remains relevant in our own world of widening economic gaps. The philosophical implications of time travel abound, challenging readers to consider the consequences of tampering with time's delicate threads. Wells' exploration of these themes has influenced subsequent literature and media, solidifying time travel as a beloved trope in the sci-fi canon.

These iconic books remind us that science fiction is more than escapism; it's a mirror reflecting our hopes, fears, and the curious dance between what is and what could be. As we close this chapter, consider how these visionary works continue to shape our understanding of technology and society, offering a lens through which we view our ever-changing world.

Your Words Matter More Than You Think

"The mind is not a vessel to be filled but a fire to be kindled."

— Plutarch

Have you ever thought about how a simple action can make someone smile? That's the magic of giving back. Let's spread that magic!

Imagine someone out there, curious about fun, quirky, and mind-blowing facts—just like you were before picking up this book. They're wondering, *"Is this the one?"* Your review can guide them to discover the joy of trivia in the most entertaining way.

My mission is simple: to make learning trivia exciting and accessible for everyone. But we need your help to keep that mission alive and growing.

When you leave a review, you're doing more than sharing your opinion—you're helping someone:

- Find their new favorite icebreaker at parties.
- Discover a hobby that makes their mornings brighter.
- Connect with friends over jaw-dropping, laugh-out-loud facts.
- Ignite curiosity in a way that inspires them every day.

It takes less than a minute, but your kind words could make a world of difference.

Would you help someone just like you—curious about trivia but unsure where to start?

Your review can be the difference. It costs nothing and takes less than a minute but could change someone's trivia journey.

- Your review could help one more reader discover the thrill of mind-bending facts.
- Your review could help one more trivia lover connect with their passion.
- Your review could help one more friend wow their crowd with unforgettable fun.

Ready to help? Just scan the QR code below and share your thoughts about *Mind-Bending Trivia for Adults*.

You're not just leaving a review—you're creating a spark of curiosity and fun for someone else. Thank you for being part of this trivia-loving community!

If you love helping others, you're my kind of person. Thank you from the bottom of my heart!

Larry Solesbee

https://is.gd/Mind_Bending

Scan QR Code
with your phone camera
to leave your review on Amazon.

8

Chapter 8: Technology and the Future

Picture this: you're sitting in your living room, trying to decide whether to order pizza or tacos for dinner. Suddenly, your refrigerator chimes in, recommending a salad because it noticed a slight uptick in your cholesterol levels. Before you can argue, your virtual assistant reminds you of your New Year's resolution to eat healthier. Welcome to the brave new world of artificial intelligence, where even your fridge has an opinion on your diet. But how did we get here, you ask? Let's rewind to a time when AI was just a twinkle in a mathematician's eye.

Artificial intelligence, or AI, didn't spring into existence fully formed, like some digital Athena. Its roots can be traced back to the mid-20th century when British mathematician Alan Turing posed the question, "Can machines think?" Turing, with his knack for cryptography and abstract thinking, laid the groundwork for what would become AI. In the 1950s, the field gained momentum, thanks to pioneers like John McCarthy and Marvin Minsky, who organized the Dartmouth Summer Research Project on Artificial Intelligence. This gathering of bright minds attempted to teach computers to do what any human toddler could: learn, solve problems, and hopefully not throw too many tantrums when things got tough.

Fast forward to the 1990s, when IBM's Deep Blue made headlines by defeating world chess champion Garry Kasparov. It was a watershed moment, akin to watching your toaster win a Nobel Prize. Deep Blue's triumph signaled the arrival of AI as a formidable force, capable of outsmarting even the best human strategists. The 21st century brought with it the rise of machine learning and neural networks, which sounded more like sci-fi jargon than actual technology. However, these advancements allowed computers to learn from vast amounts of data, improving their ability to recognize patterns and make decisions.

Today, in 2025, AI is as omnipresent as cat videos on the internet, permeating various industries and facets of our daily lives. In healthcare, AI algorithms assist doctors in diagnosing diseases and crafting personalized treatment plans, ensuring that your medical care is as unique as your Netflix recommendations. Meanwhile, in the finance sector, AI works tirelessly to detect fraudulent transactions and optimize stock trading, safeguarding your hard-earned money from nefarious digital pickpockets. Even your daily interactions are touched by AI, as virtual assistants like Siri and Alexa manage tasks with the efficiency of a digital personal assistant, minus the coffee breaks.

Of course, with great power comes great responsibility—and a host of ethical dilemmas. As AI continues to advance, questions arise about privacy and surveillance. It's one thing for your smart speaker to know your favorite playlist, but quite another for it to eavesdrop on your conversations about Aunt Edna's questionable fruitcake. Automation also threatens job security, with machines poised to replace humans in roles that were once considered uniquely ours. And as autonomous vehicles inch closer to becoming reality, we face moral quandaries about decision-making in life-or-death situations. Should an AI prioritize the safety of its passengers or the pedestrians crossing the street? It's a dilemma that even Asimov's robots might struggle to navigate.

Looking ahead, the future of AI promises both exciting possibilities and perplexing challenges. The concept of Artificial General Intelligence (AGI)—a machine that possesses human-like cognitive abilities—remains a tantalizing prospect. Imagine AI tackling global challenges like air traffic control with the same zeal it uses to recommend cat memes. Futurists like Ray Kurzweil predict AI will revolutionize creative fields, collaborating with humans to compose symphonies and design skyscrapers. While some may fear a dystopian future where machines rule, the potential for AI to enhance human capabilities is immense.

8.1 Reflection Section: AI in Your Life

Consider the ways AI touches your day-to-day life. Does your virtual assistant keep your calendar in check, or do self-driving cars tantalize you with the promise of a hands-free commute? Reflect on the conveniences AI offers and the ethical considerations they raise. As you ponder, remember: the future is unwritten, and your thoughts and choices shape the role AI will play in your world.

8.2 Breakthroughs in Space Travel

In the grand tapestry of human adventure, space travel stands out as a shimmering thread of ambition, fueled by equal parts curiosity and a desire to conquer the final frontier. Picture this: it's 1957, and the Soviet Union is having a cosmic ball, launching Sputnik, the first artificial satellite, into orbit. While the rest of the world was still grappling with black-and-white TV, Sputnik was busy beeping its way into history, igniting the space race with a beep that echoed across the globe. Fast-forward to 1969, and you have the iconic moment when Neil Armstrong took a small step for man and a giant leap for mankind. The Apollo 11 moon landing was not just a victory in the Cold War space race but a testament to human ingenuity and the power of collaboration. But space travel isn't all moonwalks and flag plantings. Remember the Apollo 1 fire disaster? It was a harsh reminder that space exploration isn't just rocket science; it's risky business. The tragedy led to critical safety overhauls, paving the way for future missions.

The 1970s brought us the saga of Apollo 13—a mission that was more of a cosmic nail-biter than a walk in the park. With a triumphant return against all odds, it became the stuff of Hollywood legend, where duct tape and determination saved the day. Then came the era of the space shuttle, a reusable marvel that promised to make space as accessible as a weekend getaway. But it wasn't all smooth sailing. The Challenger and Columbia disasters served as painful reminders of the thin line between daring and disaster. Yet, from these trials, the International Space Station (ISS) emerged, a floating testament to international cooperation and the enduring dream of living among the stars. Today, the ISS hosts astronauts from around the world, a space-bound United Nations where zero gravity meetings are the norm.

Enter the age of modern space missions, where robots and rockets redefine our cosmic understanding. NASA's Mars Rover missions, with Curiosity and Perseverance, have been the robotic pioneers, trundling across Martian landscapes, sniffing for signs of ancient life. These rovers are like the ultimate all-terrain vehicles, except instead of mud, they deal with Martian dust storms and the occasional cosmic ray. Meanwhile, SpaceX has been busy revolutionizing space travel with its reusable rockets. The Falcon Heavy launch was a spectacle to behold, with boosters returning to Earth like synchronized swimmers, gracefully landing upright on platforms that seemed impossibly small.

Let's not forget the Parker Solar Probe, which dared to venture closer to the sun than any spacecraft before, studying solar winds and other phenomena that could enlighten us about our fiery neighbor. And while the Hubble Space Telescope has had its share of glitches, its successor, the James Webb Space Telescope, promises to peer even deeper into the cosmic past, unveiling secrets of the universe's infancy. Think of it as Hubble's bigger, better cousin—one with a flair for the dramatic and a penchant for infrared.

The rise of commercial space travel has turned science fiction into reality, with companies like SpaceX, Blue Origin, and Virgin Galactic vying to take you on a cosmic joyride. Space tourism is no longer a pipe dream; it's a reality for those with deep pockets and a thirst for adventure. Private investment has fueled innovations, with asteroid mining and space colonization no longer confined to the pages of Asimov or Clarke. Picture yourself sipping a Martian mojito on a space colony, pondering the meaning of life while gazing at Earth from a million miles away.

Looking to the future, NASA's Artemis program aims to return humans to the moon, not just for a visit but to establish a lunar foothold. Plans for manned missions to Mars by the 2030s are also in the works, with the possibility of space habitats and long-term living under distant stars. International collaborations continue to be key, with agencies pooling resources and expertise to push the boundaries of what's possible. In this era of cosmic exploration, space travel is a testament to what can be achieved when imagination meets determination, and when humans dare to dream beyond the blue sky.

8.3 Here's a list of 50 common items invented or significantly popularized in the past 50 years, covering a range of technological, lifestyle, and everyday innovations:

1. Personal Computers (1970s)
2. Post-it Notes (1974)
3. Digital Cameras (1975)
4. MRI Machines (1977)
5. Walkman (1979)
6. Camcorders (1983)
7. DNA Fingerprinting (1984)
8. 3D Printing Technology (1984)
9. Disposable Contact Lenses (1987)
10. GPS for Public Use (1980s)
11. Electric Toothbrushes (1980s, popularized in 2000s)
12. World Wide Web (1991)
13. Text Messaging (SMS) (1992)
14. DVDs (1995)
15. Hybrid Cars (1997)
16. Bluetooth Technology (1999)
17. Digital Video Recorders (DVRs) (1999/2000s)
18. Wi-Fi (1999/2000s)
19. USB Flash Drives (2000)
20. Camera Phones (2000)
21. Biodegradable Plastics (2000s)
22. Reusable Water Bottles (2000s)
23. LED Light Bulbs (2000s)
24. iPods (2001)

25. Streaming Services (2006)
26. DNA Ancestry Kits (2007)
27. Blockchain Technology (2008)
28. Ride-sharing Apps (2009)
29. Tablets (2010)
30. Smart Speakers (2010s)
31. Portable Solar Chargers (2010s)
32. Smart Plugs (2010s)
33. Electric Scooters (2010s)
34. Electric Bicycles (2010s)
35. Home Security Cameras (2010s)
36. Smart Door Locks (2010s)
37. Air Fryers (2010s)
38. Smart Glasses (2010s/2020s)
39. Smart Thermostats (2011)
40. Digital Assistants (2011)
41. Streaming Devices (2013)
42. Selfie Sticks (2014)
43. Smartwatches (2014)
44. Bluetooth Headphones (2015)
45. Wireless Charging Pads (2017)
46. Foldable Smartphones (2019)
47. Reusable Face Masks (2020s)
48. Telemedicine Platforms (2020s)
49. Self-Driving Cars (2020s)
50. NFTs (2021)

9

Chapter 9: Science Oddities

Imagine walking through a dense jungle, when suddenly, you spot an octopus lounging in a tree. Before you rush to call the Guinness World Records, let me assure you: this isn't an escapee from a marine biology lab. Instead, it's a testament to the mind-boggling adaptability of the animal kingdom, where creatures employ the most bizarre strategies to survive and thrive. Welcome to a chapter where the improbable is possible and nature's oddities are the stars of the show.

Consider the octopus, nature's own version of the Swiss Army knife, with its unparalleled ability to blend into the environment. These cephalopods are the ultimate masters of disguise, capable of changing both color and texture faster than you can say "Where did it go?" Their skin contains specialized cells called chromatophores, which expand and contract to display different colors and patterns. This allows them to match their surroundings with astonishing precision, whether it's a rocky ocean floor or a coral reef. However, the mimic octopus takes this talent to a whole new level by impersonating other sea creatures like lionfish, flatfish, and even sea snakes. It's as if the octopus has a closet full of Halloween costumes, each more convincing than the last, ready to baffle both predators and prey alike.

In the realm of mimicry, the viceroy butterfly has perfected the art of imitation to avoid becoming lunch. It bears a striking resemblance to the monarch butterfly, which is toxic to predators. This clever bit of mimicry, known as Batesian mimicry, allows the viceroy to benefit from the monarch's bad reputation, deterring hungry birds from making a viceroy-shaped snack. And let's not overlook the enigmatic leaf-tailed gecko. This master of disguise looks so much like a dead leaf that even Mother Nature might mistake it for garden debris. With its leafy appendages and cryptic patterning, the gecko becomes nearly invisible against the forest floor, leaving predators scratching their heads and questioning their eyesight.

When it comes to surviving extreme environments, tardigrades, also known as water bears, have earned a reputation as the indestructible champions of the microscopic world. These tiny creatures can withstand conditions that would make even the hardiest adventurers quiver. They survive extreme temperatures, high radiation levels, and even the vacuum of space. Tardigrades achieve this feat by entering a state called cryptobiosis, where they essentially dry out and shut down their metabolic processes until conditions improve. It's like nature's version of hitting the pause button, allowing them to endure the most hostile environments the universe can throw their way.

Arctic fish, on the other hand, have developed a remarkable trick to survive freezing waters. They produce antifreeze proteins that prevent their blood from turning into ice. These proteins bind to ice crystals and inhibit their growth, ensuring the fish remain fluid and functional even when temperatures plummet. It's a biological antifreeze that allows them to swim gracefully through icy waters, while the rest of us are still fumbling with our winter coats.

In the depths of the ocean, where pressure would crush the average submarine like a tin can, deep-sea creatures like the anglerfish thrive. These fish have adapted to high-pressure environments by developing flexible bodies and unique buoyancy mechanisms. The anglerfish, with its bioluminescent lure, attracts prey in the pitch-black depths, demonstrating that even in the most extreme conditions, life finds a way to not just survive, but to glow.

Nature's reproductive strategies can often seem like the plot of a soap opera—full of twists, turns, and jaw-dropping surprises. Take the cuckoo bird, for instance, which has perfected the art of deception. Instead of building a nest and raising its young, the cunning cuckoo lays its eggs in the nests of other birds. The unsuspecting host then raises the cuckoo chick as its own, blissfully unaware of the ruse. It's the ultimate act of avian espionage, where the cuckoo gets all the benefits of parenthood without any of the responsibilities.

Certain spider species have taken a more dramatic approach to reproduction, with sexual cannibalism as a feature of their love life. In these species, the female often consumes the male after mating, providing a nutritious meal that helps her produce more offspring. It's nature's way of ensuring the male's genetic contribution goes the extra mile, albeit at the cost of his own existence.

Clownfish, those colorful denizens of the reef, have developed a fascinating reproductive strategy known as hermaphroditism. In clownfish society, the largest fish in a group is the female, while all others are male. If the female dies, the largest male undergoes a sex change and becomes the new female, ensuring the continuity of the family line. It's a fluid approach to gender roles that would make even the most progressive human communities take note.

The lancet liver fluke, meanwhile, has a life cycle that sounds like a script from a science fiction thriller. This parasitic worm requires multiple hosts to complete its life cycle, including snails, ants, and grazing mammals. By manipulating the behavior of its ant host, the fluke ensures its transmission to the next host, showcasing a complex interplay between parasite and host that defies easy explanation.

In the realm of sensory superpowers, the animal kingdom doesn't disappoint. The platypus, a creature so peculiar that scientists once thought it was a hoax, possesses an extraordinary ability to detect electric fields. Using electroreceptors in its bill, the platypus can sense the faint electrical signals produced by the muscle contractions of its prey, allowing it to hunt with precision in murky waters. It's an electrifying talent that turns the platypus into a formidable predator, even when visibility is low.

Bats and dolphins have mastered the art of echolocation, using sound waves to navigate and hunt in complete darkness. By emitting high-frequency sounds and analyzing the echoes that bounce back, these animals create a detailed sonic map of their surroundings. It's a bit like nature's sonar, allowing them to pinpoint the location of prey or obstacles with uncanny accuracy.

The mantis shrimp, with its vibrant colors and complex eyes, possesses a visual system that would make any superhero jealous. While humans have three types of color receptors, the mantis shrimp boasts up to sixteen. This extraordinary visual capability allows it to perceive ultraviolet light and detect polarized light, a skill that enhances its ability to communicate, hunt, and avoid predators in a complex underwater environment.

Migratory birds, those tireless travelers of the skies, rely on magnetic navigation to find their way across continents. These birds possess specialized cells that contain magnetite, a mineral that helps them detect Earth's magnetic field. With this internal compass, they can navigate vast distances with remarkable precision, returning to the same breeding grounds year after year.

And let's not forget our canine companions, whose heightened senses of smell and hearing make them invaluable allies in search and rescue operations. Dogs can detect scents at incredibly low concentrations, enabling them to track missing persons, locate contraband, and even sniff out medical conditions. Their acute hearing allows them to pick up sounds beyond the range of human perception, making them keen observers of their environment.

As we explore these unbelievable adaptations, it's clear that nature's creativity knows no bounds. From camouflage to extreme survival, unique reproduction to sensory superpowers, the animal kingdom offers a treasure trove of oddities that continue to captivate and inspire.

9.1 The Mysteries of Dark Matter

Imagine trying to solve a jigsaw puzzle with a blindfold on, where most pieces are missing, and you can only feel their shapes. Welcome to the world of dark matter—an enigmatic component of the universe that refuses to be seen yet pulls cosmic strings like a galactic puppeteer. Dark matter doesn't emit, absorb, or reflect light, which makes it about as visible as a ninja in the dead of night. Despite its invisibility, it's crucial for explaining gravitational effects across the universe. Without it, galaxies would spin apart like a DJ's turntable gone rogue. While dark energy is busy pushing the universe to expand, dark matter is the cosmic glue holding it all together.

The clues pointing to dark matter's existence are like cosmic breadcrumbs. For starters, galaxy rotation curves have puzzled astronomers for decades. Observations show that stars at a galaxy's edge orbit at similar speeds as those near the center, defying what you'd expect if only visible matter were involved. It's as if galaxies are riding on a cosmic merry-go-round, with dark matter providing the extra oomph to keep everything from flying off. Then there's gravitational lensing, where light from distant objects bends around massive structures, revealing a hidden mass we can't see. It's a bit like using invisible magnifying glasses that make the universe's mass display its secrets. Add to this the cosmic microwave background radiation, which offers a snapshot of the early universe, hinting at dark matter's pivotal role in shaping the cosmos.

Detecting dark matter is akin to searching for a black cat in a coal cellar at midnight. Scientists have suited up with their best detective gear, launching a series of experiments to catch this elusive quarry. The Large Hadron Collider, a behemoth of a machine, smashes particles together at breakneck speeds, hoping to produce dark matter particles by accident. It's like hosting a cosmic demolition derby and hoping a mysterious guest shows up. Meanwhile, the Cryogenic Dark Matter Search (CDMS) takes a more chilled approach, using ultra-cold detectors deep underground to capture faint signals from dark matter interactions. Think of it as trying to catch whispers in a library full of shouting children. And let's not forget the Fermi Gamma-ray Space Telescope, which scans the skies for gamma rays that might betray dark matter's presence. It's like looking for cosmic fireworks to illuminate the universe's darkest corners.

Theories abound as scientists attempt to explain dark matter's elusive nature. One popular idea involves Weakly Interacting Massive Particles (WIMPs), which are, as the name suggests, not very sociable. These particles are thought to interact with regular matter through gravity and the weak nuclear force, making them both massive and maddeningly aloof. Then there are axions, hypothetical particles that could also account for dark matter, slipping through the universe like ethereal whispers. Modified Newtonian Dynamics (MOND) offers an alternative perspective, suggesting that we might need to tweak our understanding of gravity to explain the missing mass. And let's not overlook sterile neutrinos, a potential dark matter candidate that might be lurking in the shadows, too shy to engage with the rest of the universe.

Dark matter remains one of the great mysteries of modern physics, a reminder that the universe still holds secrets as vast as the cosmos itself. Scientists continue to chase these cosmic phantoms, employing creativity and technology in their quest. Who knows what revelations await once we finally unravel the mystery of dark matter? Until then, it remains a tantalizing riddle, out there in the depths of space, just beyond the reach of human understanding.

9.2 Strange Scientific Experiments

The annals of science are peppered with experiments so peculiar they seem plucked from a mad scientist's diary. Take Ivan Pavlov, for instance, who turned the humble dog into a symbol of classical conditioning. Pavlov's dogs drooled not just at the sight of food, but at the sound of a bell that heralded their meals. It's a

tale as old as time—or at least as old as the turn of the 20th century—where dogs became more Pavlovian than canine, salivating on cue as Pavlov jotted down notes, perhaps wondering if he should switch to a career in dinner theater.

Fast forward to the 1970s, and we land in the midst of the Stanford prison experiment, where a psychology professor had the bright idea to simulate a prison environment in the basement of Stanford University. Let's just say it didn't end with everyone singing "Kumbaya." The experiment spiraled out of control, with participants so deeply immersed in their roles as guards and prisoners that it had to be terminated early. This cautionary tale taught us that humans, when given authority, might just start channeling their inner prison warden faster than you can say "ethical implications."

Meanwhile, Nikola Tesla, the original mad scientist, was busy electrifying the world—literally. Tesla's experiments with high-voltage, high-frequency power were as shocking as they were groundbreaking. Picture lightning bolts zipping through the air in Tesla's lab, making the place look like Thor's vacation home. Tesla dreamt of wireless power transmission, aiming to light up cities without a single wire. While his grand vision didn't quite pan out, his work laid the groundwork for modern electricity, proving that sometimes you have to think outside the box—or the power grid.

John Lilly, on the other hand, ventured into the realm of dolphin communication, convinced that humans could converse with these aquatic acrobats. Lilly's experiments involved trying to teach dolphins to speak English, which, unsurprisingly, didn't result in any dolphins reciting Shakespeare. However, it did spark interest in animal communication and consciousness, even if the dolphins were probably just wondering when they'd get their next fish.

In the present day, science continues to push boundaries with experiments like those conducted at the Large Hadron Collider. This colossal machine smashes particles together at mind-bending speeds, all in pursuit of the elusive Higgs boson, also known as the "God particle." It's a bit like playing cosmic bumper cars, but with far more at stake than just a few fender benders. The discovery of the Higgs boson in 2012 confirmed theories about how particles acquire mass, marking a monumental achievement in particle physics.

Gene editing, particularly with CRISPR technology, is another marvel of modern science. This tool allows scientists to edit DNA with precision, like a molecular scalpel. Researchers have used CRISPR to study gene function and explore potential therapies for genetic disorders. While the technology holds great promise, it also raises ethical questions about the extent to which we should tinker with the blueprint of life.

The double-slit experiment, one of quantum physics' most famous demonstrations, continues to baffle and intrigue. By showing that particles can behave like waves, it challenges our understanding of reality itself. Even more mind-boggling is the fact that particles seem to "choose" their state based on observation, leaving scientists scratching their heads and questioning if the universe is merely a grand illusion—or just really good at playing hide and seek.

Creating synthetic life forms is another frontier of contemporary experimentation. Scientists have succeeded in constructing organisms with artificially designed genomes, paving the way for potential breakthroughs in medicine and biotechnology. It's like playing God on a microscopic scale, with life itself as the ultimate canvas for scientific creativity.

Science isn't always a serious affair, though. Some studies are light-hearted, like those examining how long it takes different types of cheese to melt. Imagine a lab filled with bubbling pots of fondue and scientists earnestly timing the cheese melt-off. Then there's research on music's impact on plant growth, where plants are treated to classical symphonies, and scientists debate whether Beethoven or Bach yields the best blooms.

Laughter, they say, is the best medicine, and some scientists have taken this to heart, studying its effect on pain tolerance. Participants subjected to ticklish jokes and slapstick humor reportedly experienced reduced pain, suggesting that a hearty chuckle might just be more effective than a painkiller—or at least a more entertaining alternative.

And let's not forget about our feline friends. Studies on cat behavior delve into the mysteries of why cats do what they do, be it chasing laser pointers, squeezing into impossibly small boxes, or staring intently at nothing. These experiments offer insights into the peculiar world of cats, even if the results often confirm what we already suspect: cats do as they please, and we're just along for the ride.

As our exploration of strange scientific experiments concludes, it's clear that science is a tapestry woven with curiosity, creativity, and a dash of the unexpected. These experiments remind us that the pursuit of knowledge is as much about asking bold questions as it is about seeking definitive answers. So, as we turn the page to delve into the next chapter, let's keep in mind that the greatest discoveries often start with a simple "What if?" and a willingness to explore the unknown.

10

Chapter 10: History's Hidden Gems

Picture this: you're at a dinner party, and the conversation hits a lull, as it so often does when the topic veers into the realm of politics or the weather. You, however, have a secret weapon—a veritable grenade of trivia ready to explode into the room. You lean in and casually mention that one of Hollywood's most glamorous actresses, Hedy Lamarr, wasn't just a pretty face but also the mind behind the foundation of Wi-Fi technology. That's right, the next time you're binge-watching your favorite series, you can thank Lamarr for more than just her silver screen performances. During World War II, Hedy, working alongside composer George Antheil, developed frequency-hopping spread spectrum technology. This innovation was initially intended to prevent radio-controlled torpedoes from being jammed by enemies.

While the U.S. Navy gave it a polite nod and a firm "no thanks" at the time, the tech eventually became the backbone for the wireless communication we rely on today. So the next time your Wi-Fi cuts out during a crucial scene, just remember, it's only doing what it was designed to: hopping around.

Speaking of hopping, let's jump to another inventor who might not be a household name but certainly deserves to be. Enter Elijah McCoy, whose improvements in lubrication systems were so effective that people began demanding "the real McCoy." It's a testament to his unmatched ingenuity that his name became synonymous with authenticity and quality. McCoy's automatic lubrication system kept steam engines running smoothly, reducing the need for frequent stops and manual oiling. This invention was a game-changer, especially for the burgeoning railway industry. So, next time you hear someone questioning the authenticity of a product, remember that it all traces back to an inventive mind who made trains run like clockwork.

And while we're on the subject of invention and illumination, let's shed some light on Lewis Latimer. Often overshadowed by the likes of Edison and Bell, Latimer was crucial in the development of the electric light bulb. He invented a carbon filament that made light bulbs more practical and long-lasting. Without his contributions, we might still be living in a world where candles are the primary source of light, and the phrase "burning the midnight oil" is taken quite literally. So, the next time you flip a switch, think of Latimer and the glow of innovation he brought into our lives.

Now, let's talk about inventions that were so ahead of their time that they might as well have been delivered by a time-traveling DeLorean. Nikola Tesla, the eccentric genius famous for his electrical prowess, envisioned a world powered by wireless energy transfer. Although his ideas were considered too radical for his time, they laid the groundwork for the wireless charging technologies we use today. Tesla's dream of transmitting energy through the air without wires was, quite literally, electrifying and would have possibly saved us all from the tyranny of tangled cords and dead phone batteries.

In the early days of computing, John Atanasoff laid the foundation for digital computers with his Atanasoff-Berry Computer (ABC). While not immediately recognized, his work was pivotal in shaping the future of computing. His ideas on binary arithmetic and electronic switching are now fundamental to the devices we use daily. Atanasoff's contributions remind us that sometimes, being a pioneer means not seeing the full harvest of your seeds, but knowing you've planted them in fertile ground.

Let's not forget Heron of Alexandria, whose ancient steam engine, the aeolipile, was a marvel of its time. It was a globe that rotated using steam power, a precursor to engines that would revolutionize the world much later. Heron's invention was more of a novelty in its time, but it hints at a world of steam engines that could have been, if only society had been ready for such a leap.

Women have frequently been the unsung heroes in the saga of innovation, creating tools and technologies that quietly reshape the world. Ada Lovelace, often recognized as the first computer programmer, worked with Charles Babbage on his Analytical

Engine. Her insights into algorithms laid the groundwork for modern computing, proving that sometimes, the most groundbreaking ideas come from those who dare to think differently.

Margaret Knight, meanwhile, invented the paper bag machine, revolutionizing the way we carry groceries and other items. Her invention was so significant that a man tried to steal her idea, only to be thwarted by her meticulous designs. Knight's story is a reminder that ingenuity and perseverance can outwit even the most devious of rivals.

Stephanie Kwolek's invention of Kevlar, a material five times stronger than steel, has saved countless lives by being used in bulletproof vests. Her discovery was a happy accident, demonstrating that sometimes, breakthroughs happen when you least expect them but change the world in ways you could never have imagined.

Kevlar, the brainchild of chemist Stephanie Kwolek in the 1960s at DuPont, emerged from efforts to develop a lightweight fiber for tire reinforcement. This accidental discovery happened when Kwolek experimented with polybenzamide, resulting in a solution that, unlike the typical clear mixtures, was opaque and cloudy. Intrigued, Kwolek spun the solution into fibers, unveiling their extraordinary strength and stiffness, far surpassing existing materials. This led to the patenting of Kevlar in 1974, a material distinguished by its incredible strength-to-weight ratio, thanks to its molecular structure of rigid, parallel polymer chains enabling strong hydrogen bonds. Kevlar's exceptional properties make it indispensable in various applications, from bulletproof vests and helmets, where its ability to absorb and disperse impact energy saves lives, to its use in sports equipment, aerospace, automotive, and industrial sectors for its durability and resistance to cuts and abrasions. The material's success is attributed to its unique ability to withstand tension without breaking, embodying a significant advancement in material science catalyzed by Kwolek's curiosity and perseverance. Kevlar's invention not only represents a breakthrough in polymer chemistry but also continues to have a profound impact across multiple industries, safeguarding lives and enhancing the performance of products.

Finally, we look at inventors whose creations have become so integral to everyday life that it's hard to imagine a world without them. Josephine Cochrane's dishwasher invention freed households from the tyranny of manual dishwashing, while Willis Carrier's development of modern air conditioning turned sweltering summers into bearable seasons. Mary Anderson's windshield wipers are a necessity for drivers everywhere, especially during a surprise downpour. And who could forget Velcro, inspired by burrs clinging to a dog's fur, or the microwave oven, which turned accidental radiation exposure into a culinary revolution? These inventions have seamlessly integrated into our lives, making daily tasks easier and reminding us of the power of human creativity.

10.1 Secret Societies Throughout History

Imagine a world of shadowy meetings, secret handshakes, and whispered passwords—all existing just beneath the surface of our everyday lives. Welcome to the intriguing realm of secret societies, where the line between myth and reality blurs faster than you can say "conspiracy theory." Let's start with the Freemasons, perhaps the most legendary of all secret societies. Originating in the Middle Ages, this group started as a guild for stonemasons, but it quickly evolved into a society that dabbled in architecture, politics, and the occasional social soirée. They are famous for their intricate symbols, like the square and compasses, and their penchant for keeping things just mysterious enough to fuel a thousand conspiracy theories. Their influence has been felt in everything from the design of Washington D.C. to whispers of their involvement in the American Revolution. Imagine a group of well-dressed individuals gathering in dimly lit rooms, discussing ideas that could shape the course of history or at least decide who brings snacks to the next meeting.

Now, let's wander over to the Illuminati, a name that might conjure images of shadowy figures pulling the strings of world events from behind the scenes. Founded in Bavaria in the late 1700s, this group sought enlightenment through reason and reform, aiming to cast off the chains of superstition and ignorance. Or so they claimed. Their purported goal was to create a society based on merit, free from the constraints of traditional power structures. However, their secretive nature led to their swift disbandment and an enduring reputation as the puppet masters of the globe. Today, they pop up more often in pop culture and conspiracy theories than in actual historical records, but the allure of an organization that might be orchestrating global affairs still captivates the imagination.

The Rosicrucians add a mystical twist to the mix. Emerging in the early 1600s, they combined elements of magic, alchemy, and esoteric Christianity, making them the go-to group for those seeking a little extra sparkle in their spiritual pursuits. Their mysterious rose-cross symbol represents their quest for enlightenment and the blending of the material and spiritual worlds. For centuries, they've been rumored to possess ancient wisdom and secret knowledge, making them the perfect fodder for those late-night conversations that start with, "Did you know...?"

What about those rituals and symbols, you ask? Well, the Freemasons are known for their secret handshakes and elaborate ceremonies, which, despite the rumors, do not involve sacrificing goats under a full moon. These rituals are more about fostering a sense of camaraderie and tradition than summoning ancient spirits. Meanwhile, the Rosicrucians have their rose-cross emblem, a symbol as enigmatic as the society itself. And the Illuminati? They get the all-seeing eye and pyramid, icons that pop up everywhere from dollar bills to the latest thriller novel, reminding us that sometimes, symbols take on a life of their own.

In today's world, secret societies have evolved but remain just as intriguing. Take the Bohemian Club, a group that hosts an annual gathering in the California woods, where the elite gather to discuss world affairs and, presumably, roast marshmallows. Membership is exclusive, and their meetings are shrouded in secrecy, which only adds to the aura of mystery. And then there's the Bilderberg Group, a collection of the world's most powerful figures who meet annually to discuss global issues. Of course, the agenda is kept under wraps, leading to rampant speculation about what really goes on behind closed doors.

Despite the cloak of secrecy, the Freemasons continue to hold a place in modern society. They focus on community service and charitable works, proving that sometimes, the most secretive groups have the most benevolent intentions. Their rituals and symbols may seem quaint to some, but for members, they provide a connection to a long and storied history. In a world that often feels chaotic and unpredictable, perhaps the allure of secret societies lies in their promise of order and understanding, a glimpse into a world where the answers to life's big questions are just a handshake away.

10.2 Little-Known Historical Events That Changed the World

History is filled with forgotten battles that shaped the world in ways you might never have imagined. Take the Battle of Talas, for example, a clash in 751 AD between the Abbasid Caliphate and the Tang Dynasty. This wasn't just your ordinary medieval dust-up; it was a pivotal event that led to the spread of paper-making technology from China to the Muslim world. You see, the Arabs, victorious in this skirmish, captured Chinese papermakers who unwittingly shared their secret. This knowledge spread like wildfire, revolutionizing the way information was recorded, and shared, and eventually leading to the establishment of paper mills in places like Baghdad. The humble paper became the backbone of culture and administration, proving that sometimes, the pen truly is mightier than the sword—or at least more transformative.

Now, consider the Anglo-Zanzibar War, the shortest war in history, clocking in at a brisk 38 minutes. It was essentially the geopolitical equivalent of a blink. The conflict arose when the Sultan of Zanzibar dared to annoy the British Empire by not stepping down after his predecessor's death. The British responded in the only way they knew how—by bringing gunboats to a diplomacy fight. The Sultan's palace was quickly reduced to rubble, and a new leader was installed faster than you can say "regime change." Though brief, the war demonstrated the lengths to which empires would go to maintain their influence, even if it meant a war that lasted less than most lunch breaks.

Then there's the Battle of Cajamarca, where a small band of Spanish conquistadors managed to topple the mighty Inca Empire. Armed with steel, gunpowder, and a fair amount of treachery, Francisco Pizarro and his men captured the Incan Emperor Atahualpa in 1532. This encounter wasn't just a military victory; it marked the beginning of the end for the Incas and the start of Spanish dominance in South America. The riches looted by the conquistadors fueled their empire, while the cultural upheaval reshaped the continent, creating a lasting legacy that reverberates to this day.

Treaties often have a knack for reshaping the world map, sometimes with the precision of a surgeon, other times with the flair of a toddler wielding a crayon. The Treaty of Tordesillas in 1494 is a prime example. It divided the newly discovered lands outside Europe between Spain and Portugal along a meridian, all with the Pope's blessing. This division granted Brazil to Portugal, while the rest of the Americas went to Spain, setting the stage for centuries of colonial expansion and conflict. It was an arbitrary line on a map that had colossal implications, influencing the languages, cultures, and politics of entire continents.

The Peace of Westphalia in 1648 ended the Thirty Years' War, a conflict so convoluted it makes a soap opera look straightforward. This treaty established the concept of state sovereignty, recognizing the rights of states to govern themselves without outside interference. It was a watershed moment in international relations, laying the groundwork for the modern nation-state system. Imagine a world where your next-door neighbor couldn't tell you how to mow your lawn—that's Westphalia's legacy in a nutshell.

The Adams-Onís Treaty of 1819 was another cartographic coup, where Spain ceded Florida to the United States. This deal settled border disputes between the two nations and paved the way for America's westward expansion. Florida, with its swamps and sunshine, became a U.S. territory, leaving Spain to focus on its remaining holdings in Latin America. It was a diplomatic dance that expanded America's footprint, all while ensuring that the Spanish could still vacation in the Caribbean.

Diplomacy, like a game of chess, sometimes involves moves so bizarre they belong in a comedy skit. Take the Pig War of 1859, a standoff between the U.S. and Britain over a dead pig on a tiny island in the Pacific Northwest. The pig, owned by an Irishman, dared to dig up an American farmer's potatoes, leading to its untimely demise and an international incident. Thankfully, cooler heads prevailed, and the conflict ended without a shot fired (besides the pig), proving that sometimes, wars aren't about grand ideologies but simple misunderstandings.

In Australia, the Emu War of 1932 was a battle between soldiers and emus. Yes, emus. The flightless birds were ravaging crops, and the government deployed soldiers with machine guns to control them. The emus, with their agility and numbers, outmaneuvered the military, resulting in a comical defeat. It was a lesson in humility and the limits of military power against nature's quirky challenges.

The Pastry War of 1838 between France and Mexico sounds like a culinary disagreement, but it was far more serious. A French pastry chef claimed Mexican soldiers damaged his bakery, seeking compensation. France responded aggressively, blockading Mexican ports until debts were settled. This diplomatic spat demonstrated the often absurd triggers of international conflict, where a single bakery could ignite a war.

Social movements often emerge from the shadows, leaving indelible marks on society long after their inception. The Luddites, for example, were not just technophobes smashing machines; they were skilled workers protesting the misuse of technology during the Industrial Revolution. They fought for fair labor practices and quality craftsmanship, a struggle that echoes in modern debates about technology's role in the workforce.

The Bonus Army March of 1932 saw World War I veterans descend on Washington, D.C., demanding early bonus payments during the Great Depression. Their efforts highlighted the plight of struggling veterans and influenced future policies on veterans' benefits. It was a testament to the power of collective action, even when met with resistance.

The Seneca Falls Convention in 1848 was a groundbreaking moment in the women's rights movement. Organized by pioneers like Elizabeth Cady Stanton, it marked the beginning of a long struggle for gender equality. The convention's Declaration of Sentiments outlined grievances and set the stage for future advancements in women's rights, a legacy that continues to inspire activists.

As we close this chapter, remember that history is not just a series of events but a tapestry of interconnected stories. Each battle, treaty, incident, and movement has played a role in shaping the world we know today, reminding us that sometimes, the most significant changes start with the smallest ripples.

10.3 Time-out for a Trivia matching quiz #3

Slang Words: Can you match these words to their descriptions below?

1- Big Oof
2- Bougie
3- Bromance
4- Drip
5- Dumpster Fire
6- FOMO
7- Ghosting
8- Glamping

9- Karen

10- Sus

A- A chaotic or disastrous situation

B- A close, non-romantic friendship between men

C- A pejorative term for a middle-aged woman acting entitled or demanding.

D- An expression for a significant mistake or setback

E- expressing anxiety over missing fun or exciting events.

F- luxury camping

G- Refers to stylish clothing or accessories.

H- Something feels off or sketchy.

I- used to describe something fancy or high-class, often with irony

J- When someone suddenly cuts off all communication without explanation.

Trivia matching quiz answers

1-D, 2-I, 3-B, 4-G, 5-A, 6-E, 7-J, 8-F, 9-C, 10-H

Trivia matching quiz chart in Chapter 13.4

11

Chapter 11: Strange Sports and Games

Have you ever found yourself ironing a shirt, staring out the window at the mountain you wish you were climbing instead? Now, imagine doing both at once. Welcome to the curious world of extreme ironing, where the mundane meets the thrilling in a spectacle that's as bizarre as it is captivating. This unconventional sport takes something as routine as ironing and elevates it—literally—by having participants press their garments in locations that make even the bravest adventurers pause. It's a sport that asks, "Why settle for a crumpled shirt when you can iron it on a cliff?"

11.1 The World of Extreme Ironing

The origins of extreme ironing are as quirky as the sport itself. It all began in 1997 when Phil Shaw, a Leicester native affectionately known as "Steam," decided that ironing could use

a bit more excitement. As the story goes, Shaw returned home from a hard day at work and faced the domestic drudgery of ironing. But instead of resigning himself to the monotony, he grabbed his ironing board and headed out into his garden, sparking an idea that would soon become a global phenomenon. Shaw's vision of blending the thrill of outdoor adventure with the banality of ironing struck a chord, and by 1999, he was promoting the sport internationally. The first organized competition took place in Germany in 2002, attracting 80 teams eager to showcase their pressing prowess.

So, what does one need to participate in this peculiar pastime? Surprisingly, the equipment is standard: an ironing board, an iron (electric or battery-operated for those remote locations), and items of clothing in need of a good press. But it's not just about getting those creases out; participants are judged on creativity, skill, and the quality of their ironing. It's about who can produce the best-pressed shirt while risking life and limb. Imagine scaling a rock face in England's Peak District, only to pause midway and whip out your ironing board. Or diving into a lake, bubbles rising as you diligently press a pair of trousers underwater. Some have even taken to ironing atop moving vehicles, from cars to boats, adding a whole new layer of difficulty—and hilarity—to the proceedings.

Among the sport's crowning achievements are the Extreme Ironing World Championships, where competitors face off in a test of nerves and ironing skill. It's not just about the location; it's about how well you can balance both the board and your composure in the most precarious of places. Participants have ironed at dizzying heights near Everest Base Camp and even set records for the deepest underwater ironing sessions. It's a spectacle that leaves spectators in awe and participants with perfectly pressed shirts—or at least the best-pressed shirts ever seen on a mountainside.

The media has taken notice, with extreme ironing finding its way into major outlets like The Wall Street Journal and ESPN. Documentaries, such as "Extreme Ironing: Pressing for Victory," have chronicled the sport, capturing the dedication and eccentricity of its participants. This sport, once a quirky hobby, has sparked a community of enthusiasts who gather to share their passion for pressing in the most unlikely of places. It's an activity that embraces the absurdity of modern life, turning a chore into a daring adventure. Whether you're an adrenaline junkie or just someone who wants a more exciting way to de-wrinkle your wardrobe, extreme ironing proves that even the most routine tasks can become extraordinary.

11.2 Quirky Board Games from Around the Globe

Picture this: a dusty, ancient room filled with the echoes of ancient laughter and the clatter of dice. This is where the Royal Game of Ur, one of the oldest known board

games, was played in ancient Mesopotamia. Imagine kings and commoners alike huddled over a beautifully carved board, plotting their next move with the same intensity you'd expect from a modern chess grandmaster. Fast-forward to Egypt, where Senet was the game of choice. Found in the tombs of pharaohs, this game was more than mere entertainment; it was thought to guide souls to the afterlife. The Vikings, not to be outdone, had their own strategic pastime: Hnefatafl. Much like chess, this game involved a king and his defenders battling against attackers, perhaps offering a brief respite from pillaging and plundering. Meanwhile, in India, Pachisi was the predecessor of what you might recognize today as Ludo. There are many Western versions of Pachisi, including Parchís in Spain, Parcheesi in the United States, and Uckers, a naval version of Ludo. In France, the game is called jeu des petits chevaux, which means "game of little horses". In Germany, it's known as Mensch ärgere Dich nicht. Players navigated their pieces across a cross-shaped board, using cowrie shells as dice, in a game that was as much about luck as it was about strategy.

Modern board games have taken a turn for the whimsical, embracing themes and mechanics that would make our ancient ancestors scratch their heads in amusement. Take "Exploding Kittens," for instance—a game where players draw cards until someone pulls an exploding kitten and, well, explodes. It's Russian Roulette with a furry twist, and it's as absurd as it is entertaining. Then there's "Secret Hitler," a game that combines hidden roles with social deduction, encouraging players to deceive and manipulate their way to victory. It's like a political thriller, except with more laughter and fewer campaign finance scandals. "Mice and Mystics" offers a cooperative adventure where players are transformed into mice, battling their way through a storybook world filled with danger and cheese. And if you're into schadenfreude, "Gloom" is the game for you. Here, the goal is to make your characters as miserable as possible before they meet their untimely demise. It's a game where the worse your luck, the better your score.

Rewind to the late 20th century, a golden age for board games that brought us icons like Monopoly and Sorry, games as familiar as that one mysterious key on your key ring. Monopoly, with its endless cycle of buying, trading, and bankrupting your friends, is a rite of passage for anyone who's ever dreamed of real estate domination. Then there's Sorry and Chutes and Ladders, games that taught valuable lessons about the capricious nature of fate— one minute you're on top, the next you're sliding down to start all over. Card games like Canasta and Pinochle were staples at many a family gathering, while dice games like Yahtzee brought out the competitive streak in everyone from Grandma to the family dog.

Venturing beyond our borders, we find games that are beloved in their native lands yet often unknown elsewhere. "Carrom" is a tabletop game from South Asia, although I remember playing Carrom as a kid in the early 1960s in Southern California. It combines the precision of billiards with the simplicity of flicking coins. It's a game of skill, strategy, and patience, perfect for those who enjoy a good challenge. Over in East Asia, "Go" reigns supreme—a game so strategic and complex that it makes chess look like a casual Sunday crossword puzzle. In Mexico, "Lotería" is a bingo-like game, but with beautifully illustrated cards that capture the vibrancy of Mexican culture. In Canada, "Crokinole" offers a dexterous challenge, where players flick discs across a circular board, aiming for the center while avoiding their opponents' pieces.

For those who prefer a personal touch, DIY board games offer endless possibilities. Enthusiasts create custom versions of "Monopoly," replacing Park Place with local landmarks or inside jokes that only their closest friends will understand. Homemade trivia games based on family history add a nostalgic twist, turning forgotten anecdotes into competitive fun. Some fans even handcraft "Settlers of Catan" with personalized tiles, creating a version that's as unique as the players themselves. And then there are games made from repurposed materials, like bottle caps and recycled paper, proving that creativity knows no bounds.

11.3 Bizarre Olympic Events

Picture this: a group of athletes, muscles taut, faces strained, locked in a fierce battle of tug-of-war. Yes, you read that right. Tug-of-war was once an Olympic event, included in the early 20th century Games. Teams of burly men from various nations would pull with all their might, vying for a gold medal in a sport more commonly associated with summer picnics. Alas, like bell-bottoms and disco music, it eventually fell out of favor and was discontinued after 1920. But just imagine the drama of a tug-of-war final, with the whole world watching and cheering as though their national pride depended on it.

Then there's solo synchronized swimming, which sounds like the setup for a punchline. How can one synchronize with oneself? It's an Olympic puzzle that makes you question the very nature of synchronization. Though it only graced the Games for a short period, it left audiences scratching their heads and wondering if they'd wandered into a surrealist art exhibit by mistake. And let's not forget the short-lived spectacle of live pigeon shooting in the 1900 Paris Olympics. Competitors aimed to hit as many pigeons as possible, a feat that, unsurprisingly, didn't win many fans and was never repeated.

In the 1904 Games, divers competed in the Plunge for Distance, an event that involved diving into a pool and gliding underwater as far as possible without any strokes. It was less about speed and more about channeling your inner otter. This event quietly vanished, leaving us to ponder how many of these athletes were just holding their breath and hoping for the best.

The Olympics have also seen their share of demonstration sports, which are like auditions for the real Games. Take korfball, for instance, a mixed-gender sport that resembles basketball but with a unique twist. It's played on a rectangular court with two baskets but emphasizes cooperation between male and female players, making it a progressive addition to any sporting event. Then there's the graceful art of gliding, demonstrated in 1936, where athletes soared silently through the sky, showcasing the serenity and skill of aerial navigation. Basque pelota, with its fast-paced action and rich cultural roots in Spain and France, has also made appearances as a demonstration sport. And who can forget ski ballet? This winter wonder combined the elegance of dance with the thrill of skiing, creating a performance that was as mesmerizing as it was peculiar.

Modern Olympic events have not shied away from the unconventional either. Trampoline gymnastics, introduced in Sydney 2000, brings a whole new meaning to bouncing back. Athletes flip and twist high in the air, combining the acrobatics of gymnastics with the fun of a backyard trampoline. Canoe slalom, another adrenaline-pumping sport, has competitors navigating turbulent whitewater courses, battling both the elements and the clock. It's like a rollercoaster without the tracks. Rhythmic gymnastics, with its ribbons, hoops, and balls, marries the grace of ballet with the physicality of gymnastics, creating a spectacle that is both captivating and complex. And let's not overlook skateboarding and break dancing. These new entries bring street culture to the Olympics, challenging traditional notions of what constitutes a sport and proving that athleticism comes in many forms.

As we look to the future, the possibilities for Olympic events are as limitless as the athletes' imaginations. E-sports, with their global fanbase and competitive nature, could soon join the ranks, merging gaming with athletics in a way that would make Pac-Man proud. Parkour, the art of fluid movement through urban landscapes, could leap from the streets to the Olympic stage, showcasing agility and creativity. Drone racing, a high-speed competition of piloting skill, might offer a technological twist to traditional races. And Ultimate Frisbee, with its growing international recognition, could bring a laid-back yet fiercely competitive edge to the Games.

In a world where sports evolve as quickly as the athletes who play them, the Olympic Games continue to surprise and delight, proving that the spirit of competition is as dynamic as ever. As we close this chapter, let's prepare to explore the next realm of trivia, where the world of mind-bending math and numbers awaits.

12

Chapter 12: Mind-Blowing Math and Numbers

If you've ever tried to split a pizza among friends without causing an existential crisis, you might appreciate the elegance of the Fibonacci sequence. This mathematical wonder starts simple enough with a pair of numbers—0 and 1. From there, each subsequent number is the sum of the two preceding it, creating a sequence that looks something like this: 0, 1, 1, 2, 3, 5, 8, 13, and so on. This sequence is named after Fibonacci, also known as Leonardo of Pisa, who introduced it to the Western world through his 1202 masterpiece "Liber Abaci." While Fibonacci might have been more interested in the mathematical implications, the sequence has far more intriguing applications, like predicting the growth of rabbit populations. Imagine a world where rabbits multiply according to a mathematical sequence— wait, that's actually our world.

The Fibonacci sequence doesn't just stop at furry creatures hopping around fields. It also manifests in the natural world in ways that make you wonder if Mother Nature had a secret love affair with math. Take a stroll through a sunflower field, and you might notice how the seeds are arranged in spirals. These patterns are not just pretty to look at—they follow the Fibonacci sequence, optimizing packing and seed distribution. Pinecones, pineapples, and even pomegranates share this mathematical artistry in their structures, boasting arrangements that follow this sequence. Then there are hurricanes, whose spiral forms mirror the Fibonacci sequence, reminding us that even the most chaotic natural phenomena have a touch of mathematical order. It's as if the universe decided to doodle with a mathematical compass.

The Fibonacci sequence is also a gateway to the golden ratio, an irrational number approximately equal to 1.6180339887. As you move through the sequence, the ratio of successive Fibonacci numbers gradually approaches this golden ratio, a phenomenon that has captured the imagination of mathematicians, artists, and architects alike. This ratio is seen in the proportions of everything from the Parthenon to your favorite Instagram filter. It's a mathematical constant that seems to have an aesthetic appeal, like that one friend who always looks good in photos no matter what. Beyond that, Fibonacci numbers have a relationship with binomial coefficients and make cameo appearances in Pascal's Triangle, proving that math is the original crossover artist.

In the modern world, Fibonacci numbers have stepped off the page and into the realm of technology and finance. They play a crucial role in computer algorithms, particularly in sorting and searching tasks. When your computer efficiently organizes your chaotic desktop files or finds that one email among a thousand, it might just have a Fibonacci sequence to thank. In the realm of finance, Fibonacci retracement levels are used in technical analysis to predict potential reversal points in asset prices. Traders, who are often portrayed as calculating risk-takers, rely on these sequences to navigate the volatile waters of financial markets. It's like using math as a crystal ball, except with fewer mystical incantations and more spreadsheets.

Visual art and architecture have long been enchanted by the Fibonacci spiral, a shape that reflects the sequence's inherent beauty. From the nautilus shell to the spiral staircases of grand old libraries, these spirals captivate with their grace and symmetry. Artists and architects have used the Fibonacci sequence to create visually pleasing and structurally sound works, proving that math isn't just for the classroom—it's also for the canvas and the construction site. Whether in the form of swirling galaxies or the meticulous design of a building facade, Fibonacci spirals remind us that math can be as much about beauty as it is about numbers.

To truly experience the allure of Fibonacci, try creating your own Fibonacci sequence. Start with a simple pair of numbers and see where they take you. Observe how quickly they grow, and marvel at the surprising complexity that arises from such a simple rule. The magic of Fibonacci is not just in the numbers themselves but in the way they reveal a hidden harmony in the world around us.

12.1 Unsolved Mathematical Mysteries

In the vast universe of mathematics, few mysteries are as tantalizing as the Riemann Hypothesis. Proposed by the German mathematician Bernhard Riemann in 1859, this hypothesis is the mathematical equivalent of a classic whodunit—except the victim is your free time and the detective is every number theorist on the planet. At its core, the Riemann Hypothesis concerns the distribution of prime numbers, those indivisible building blocks of arithmetic that seem to pop up as unpredictably as a squirrel in a flower bed. Specifically, it deals with the zeros of the Riemann zeta function, a complex mathematical function that looks like it could power a time machine if only we understood it better. Should anyone manage to prove or disprove the hypothesis, it could unlock profound insights into number theory and complex analysis, potentially solving longstanding problems and possibly breaking the internet—or at least a few mathematicians. Despite many brilliant minds working on it, the hypothesis remains just that—a hypothesis, leaving a trail of mathematicians scratching their heads and muttering about zeros on critical lines.

In contrast to the highbrow allure of the Riemann Hypothesis, the Collatz Conjecture brings a simpler, yet equally perplexing enigma to the table. Known affectionately as the "3n + 1" problem, this conjecture starts with any positive integer n. If n is even, you divide by 2; if odd, you multiply by 3 and add 1. Repeat this process, and according to the conjecture, you'll eventually reach the number 1. It's a mathematical ritual that sounds like it belongs more in a board game than in a serious mathematical discussion. Despite its straightforward rules, no one has yet found a proof that this process will always end at 1 for every starting number. The Collatz Conjecture is like that impossible-to-solve puzzle you find in a cereal box, deceptively simple yet maddeningly unsolvable. Over the years, countless mathematicians have taken a swing at it, only to find themselves caught in an endless loop of numbers and frustration, much like the sequence itself.

Then there's the P vs NP Problem, which might sound like a boxing match but is actually a fundamental question in computer science. It asks whether every problem whose solution can be quickly verified by a computer (that's NP) can also be quickly solved by a computer (that's P). To put it in everyday terms, P is like finding out your favorite song in seconds using an app, while NP is like knowing the lyrics are correct because you've checked them against the song. The implications of proving P equals NP—or not—are enormous. It could revolutionize cryptography, alter optimization techniques, and change how algorithms are designed. Imagine being able to solve puzzles, crack codes, or optimize routes in an instant. The world would be your oyster, which, incidentally, would be much easier to open if P equals NP. Despite its significance, this problem remains unsolved, much to the chagrin of computer scientists everywhere who are still waiting for their "Eureka!" moment.

Finally, the Navier-Stokes Existence and Smoothness problem stands as the granddaddy of fluid dynamics conundrums. These equations describe the motion of fluid substances like air and water, which is why they're crucial for understanding everything from weather patterns to how coffee swirls in your cup. The challenge here is to prove or disprove the existence of smooth, globally defined solutions to these equations. In simpler terms, mathematicians are trying to determine whether there will always be solutions that don't blow up into chaos. Solving this could revolutionize our understanding of turbulence, making weather forecasts more reliable, improving aircraft design, and perhaps even explaining why your showerhead always sprays water in every direction except the one you want. Despite the considerable brainpower dedicated to it, the Navier-Stokes problem continues to be as slippery as the fluids it seeks to understand.

12.2 Math in Nature: The Golden Ratio

Picture a world where numbers hold the secret to beauty and balance. This is the realm of the Golden Ratio, often represented by the Greek letter φ (phi), approximately equal to 1.6180339887. It's like the world's most exclusive club for numbers, and Phi is the glittering VIP. Known since the time of the ancient Greeks, this ratio has been the darling of mathematicians, artists, and architects alike. It pops up in the geometry of the pentagon, which is why you can find it in some of the world's most famous structures and artworks. It's as if Phi decided to make a cameo appearance in every corner of history, just to keep us guessing.

The Golden Ratio is a specific mathematical constant, approximately equal to 1.618, which is derived from the Fibonacci sequence, a series of numbers where each number is the sum of the two preceding numbers; essentially, as you progress through the Fibonacci sequence, the ratio between consecutive numbers gets increasingly closer to the Golden Ratio value.

The ancient Greeks weren't the only ones smitten with this numerical heartthrob. During the Renaissance, artists and architects couldn't get enough of it. Take the Parthenon in Athens, for instance. Its proportions echo the Golden Ratio, creating a structure that has captivated the world for centuries, much like a celebrity who somehow never ages. Leonardo da Vinci, the Renaissance man himself, used the Golden Ratio in his "Vitruvian Man" and "The Last Supper." It's like he had a secret mathematical sauce to make his art irresistible. Fast-forward to modern times, and you'll find the Golden Ratio gracing the design of the United Nations building and even the CN Tower in Toronto, Ontario, Canada. It's like the ratio has a passport to the world's most iconic landmarks, forever leaving its mark.

But the Golden Ratio doesn't just hang out in museums and architecture tours. It's woven into the very fabric of nature. Leaves, flowers, and seeds often follow this ratio, arranging themselves in spirals that optimize sunlight and space. It's like nature's way of saying, "Look, I can do math too!" Even your body is a walking testament to this ratio. The proportions between different parts of the human body often reflect the Golden Ratio, which might explain why some people are just so darn photogenic. And let's not overlook the spiral patterns in hurricanes and galaxies, as if the universe decided to doodle on a cosmic scale. Even DNA, the blueprint of life, has proportions that echo this ancient ratio, proving that math is in our very genes.

Beyond its aesthetic appeal, the Golden Ratio has some mathematical tricks up its sleeve. Its unique algebraic properties include self-similarity, meaning that if you zoom in on a spiral or a pattern that uses the Golden Ratio, you'll find the same proportions repeated over and over, like a mathematical version of a fractal. This self-similarity also finds applications in modern design and technology. User interfaces, logos, and even your favorite apps might employ the Golden Ratio to keep things looking sleek and balanced. It's the secret sauce that makes good design feel just right, even if you can't quite put your finger on why.

In the financial world, the Golden Ratio is like the mysterious oracle traders turn to for insight. It's used to predict stock price movements in technical analysis, helping traders make decisions based on patterns that align with this magical number. It's like having a crystal ball, but instead of seeing the future, you're seeing a beautifully proportioned spreadsheet. And if you're into chaos theory and fractal geometry, you'll find the Golden Ratio popping up there, too. It acts as a guide through the seemingly random, revealing a hidden order within the chaos.

As we wrap up this chapter, remember that the Golden Ratio is much more than a number. It's a bridge between math, art, nature, and even the cosmos. It's a reminder that beauty and balance are universal, and sometimes, they can be summed up with a single number. Whether you're gazing at a sunflower, admiring a painting, or navigating the stock market, the Golden Ratio is there, whispering its secrets to those who care to listen. So next time you marvel at the world around you, remember that there's math lurking beneath the surface, making everything just a little more perfect.

13

Chapter 13: Language and Words You Won't Believe Exist

Ever found yourself at a party where someone suddenly drops a word so strange that you wonder if they're casting a spell or making up their own language? Welcome to the whimsical world of unusual and rare English words, where the vocabulary is as curious as a cat in a cucumber patch. Imagine you're at a fancy dinner, and someone casually mentions they have the "collywobbles." Before you sound the alarm for a medical emergency, rest assured they're just feeling a bit anxious—likely about whether to use the salad fork or the tiny one that no one ever remembers the purpose of.

The English language, bless its heart, is a treasure trove of oddities. Take "absquatulate," for instance. This delightful verb means to leave abruptly, perhaps when you realize you've been talking to your reflection instead of your colleague at the office party. Then there's "gobbledygook," which perfectly describes the jargon-heavy emails that make you question if your coworker moonlights as a cryptographer. Feeling "lackadaisical"? That's just a fancy way of saying you're too relaxed to even muster up the enthusiasm to be lazy. And for those moments when you're accused of "lollygagging" or "dillydallying," know that it's just a playful reprimand for dawdling when you should be doing something slightly more productive, like reorganizing your sock drawer.

But where do these odd words come from? Their origins are as colorful as their meanings. Take "pneumonoultramicroscopicsilicovolcanoconiosis"—a word so long it could rival a CVS receipt. It was coined to humorously describe a lung disease caused by inhaling fine silicate or quartz dust, possibly invented by someone with a penchant for long words and short jokes. "Flummox," a word that leaves you feeling, well, flummoxed, might derive from the dialectal "flummock," meaning to confuse. Meanwhile, "bumfuzzle" sounds like the result of a toddler creating a new language, but it's actually a blend of "bum" (to make a mess) and "fuzzle" (to confuse), illustrating the chaotic charm of English etymology.

As if navigating these words isn't challenging enough, English throws in a few curveballs with peculiar pronunciations. Take "colonel." Written as if it's a relative of "colon," but pronounced "ker-nul," it's a word that laughs in the face of phonetics. Then there's "Worcestershire," which, despite its daunting spelling, is simply "woos-ter-sheer," though many still opt for the safer "that sauce." "Epitome" might look like it should rhyme with "gnome," but it's "ih-pit-uh-mee" instead. And "chthonic," a word that sounds like a sneeze, is pronounced "thon-ik." These words are the linguistic equivalent of a funhouse mirror—what you see is not quite what you get.

Finally, we venture into the realm of words with bizarre meanings, where English truly embraces the eccentric. "Defenestration" might sound like a complex medical procedure, but it's actually the act of throwing someone out of a window—a word that's oddly specific yet strangely satisfying. And if you've ever managed to "quomodocunquize," congratulations, because that means you've found a way to make money by any means necessary, perhaps by selling your collection of rare pogs. In chess, "zugzwang" refers to a situation where any move will worsen your position—a word that might also apply to your predicament when asked if you've remembered your partner's birthday. Lastly, "bloviate" describes speaking pompously or boastfully, a word best used to describe your uncle's tales that grow taller with each retelling.

13.1 Bonus list of words with bizarre meanings.

1. **Bamboozled**: To be deceived, tricked, or confused by someone, often in a playful or sneaky manner.
2. **Canoodle**: To engage in affectionate behavior like cuddling, hugging, or kissing.
3. **Codswallop**: Nonsense or foolish talk; something that is silly or not true.
4. **Dingleberry**: This can refer to either a small, annoying piece of dried fecal matter caught in hair or, informally, a foolish or inept person.
5. **Discombobulated**: Confused, disoriented, or unsettled.

6. **Flabbergasted**: Extremely surprised or shocked; astonished.
7. **Flibbertigibbet**: A frivolous, talkative, or flighty person who is often seen as silly or gossipy.
8. **Kerfuffle**: A commotion, fuss, or disturbance, usually caused by a disagreement or confusion.
9. **Malarky**: Silly talk, nonsense, or something that is insincere or exaggerated.
10. **Nincompoop**: A foolish or silly person.
11. **Persnickety**: Overly fussy, picky, or concerned with trivial details.
12. **Poppycock**: Nonsense or something that is absurd and untrue.
13. **Pumpernickel**: A type of dark, dense rye bread, originally from Germany.
14. **Shenanigans**: Mischievous or playful activities, often involving trickery or pranks.
15. **Skedaddle**: To leave quickly or run away in a hurry.
16. **Thingamajig**: A placeholder term used when the actual name of an object is forgotten or unknown.
17. **Whatchamacallit**: Another placeholder term similar to "thingamajig," used for an item whose name one cannot recall.
18. **Whippersnapper**: A young, inexperienced person who is perceived as overconfident or presumptuous.

13.2 Did You Know These Things Had Names?

1. The space between your eyebrows is called a glabella.

2. The way it smells after the rain is called petrichor.
3. The plastic or metallic coating at the end of your shoelaces is called an aglet.
4. The rumbling of the stomach is called a wamble.
5. The cry of a newborn baby is called a vagitus.
6. The prongs on a fork are called tines.
7. The sheen or light that you see when you close your eyes and press your hands on them is called phosphenes.
8. The tiny plastic table placed in the middle of a pizza box is called a box tent.
9. The day after tomorrow is called overmorrow.
10. Your tiny toe or finger is called minimus.
11. The wired cage that holds the cork in a bottle of champagne is called an agraffe.
12. The 'na na na' and 'la la la', which don't really have any meaning in the lyrics of any song, are called vocables.
13. When you combine an exclamation mark with a question mark (like this ?!), it is referred to as an interrobang.
14. The space between your nostrils is called columella nas
15. The armhole in clothes, where the sleeves are sewn, is called armscye.
16. The condition of finding it difficult to get out of bed in the morning is called dysania.
17. Illegible handwriting is called griffonage.
18. The dot over an "i" or a "j" is called a tittle.
19. That utterly sick feeling you get after eating or drinking too much is called crapulence.
20. The metallic device used to measure your feet at the shoe store is called the Brannock device.

These words and their peculiarities remind us of the playful nature of language. They're the verbal equivalent of a hidden Easter egg in a video game—unexpected, delightful, and just a little bit strange.

13.3 Untranslatable Words from Other Cultures

Imagine sitting in a cozy chair, wrapped in a blanket, sipping hot cocoa, while the rain patters softly against the window. This scene might evoke a sense of "hygge," a Danish concept that embodies cozy contentment and conviviality. It's not just a word; it's a lifestyle choice, like deciding to wear socks with sandals. Meanwhile, picture yourself at a party, secretly reveling as someone else trips over their own feet and spills a drink. That little twinge of pleasure is "schadenfreude," a German term that perfectly captures the delight in another's misfortune, even if you'd never admit it out loud. Over in Japan, the concept of "wabi-sabi" invites you to embrace the beauty of imperfection, like appreciating a chipped mug that holds memories, or the artfully crooked line of your last DIY project. And if you've ever admired the sunlight filtering through leaves during a walk in the park, you've experienced "komorebi," a Japanese word that captures this specific and fleeting beauty.

In Portugal, "saudade" captures a profound longing for something or someone absent, a feeling so deep it almost aches. It's the emotion behind listening to a sad song on repeat, even when you've moved on. Imagine "gezelligheid," a Dutch word that describes the warmth of being with loved ones, the kind of coziness that makes you feel like the world is a little less daunting. Across the globe in the Nguni Bantu languages, "ubuntu" embodies the philosophy that our humanity is interconnected, a reminder that no person is an island, even if they sometimes wish they were. Then there's "mamihlapinatapai," a Yaghan word from Tierra del Fuego, which describes the shared, silent look between two people who both wish the other would initiate something they both desire. It's the epitome of romantic tension, captured in a single, wonderfully specific term.

Let's explore words that precisely capture unique situations. If you've ever felt secondhand embarrassment watching someone bomb a presentation, you've experienced "pena ajena," a Spanish term for the cringe you feel on their behalf. Meanwhile, the Tagalog word "gigil" describes the overwhelming urge to pinch something cute, like a chubby baby or an adorable puppy, though it might not appreciate it. In Indonesia, when a joke is so terrible it becomes funny simply because it's so bad, it's called "jayus"—a term that could describe many a stand-up routine. These words capture experiences so specific that even the most verbose English speaker would struggle to articulate them without resorting to elaborate pantomime.

Translating these words can be as tricky as trying to assemble flat-pack furniture without instructions. Cultural context is the secret sauce that gives words their flavor, and without it, translations can fall flat. Take idiomatic expressions, for example. They're the linguistic equivalent of inside jokes; without the context, they're just confusing. This is why translators are like linguistic detectives, piecing together meaning from cultural clues. When words evolve, their meanings can shift, leaving translators to play catch-up with a language that's constantly in motion. This evolution means translators need to be part historian, part poet, and all patience. It's a balancing act between preserving the original flavor and making it palatable to a new audience, much like trying to explain the appeal of Vegemite to someone who isn't Australian.

13.4 The Evolution of Slang Over Time

Slang is like the wild child of language, never sitting still and constantly reinventing itself. Take a moment to time-travel back to the 1920s, an era when everything was "the bee's knees." This quirky term was the pinnacle of praise, used to describe someone or something outstanding. Fast-forward to the groovy 1960s, where "groovy" was the word of the day, epitomizing everything excellent and fashionable, from bell-bottoms to flower power. The 1980s brought us "rad," short for radical, which was used to describe anything impressive or cool, whether it was a skateboard trick or a neon jacket. And in the 2010s, we were all about things being "cray," a snappy shorthand for crazy, capturing the wild essence of the digital age. Or in 2024, someone who is "Riz" has charisma. Each decade has its own linguistic icons, reflecting the spirit and culture of its time, like a verbal time capsule.

Pop culture has always been a fertile breeding ground for slang, with music, movies, and television leading the charge. Hip-hop culture, in particular, has given us gems like "bling" for flashy jewelry and "dope" for something exceptionally cool. TV shows have also played their part in shaping our vernacular. Consider "The Simpsons," which gifted us with "D'oh!"—a word that needs no explanation but fits perfectly in moments of exasperation. Then there's Joey from "Friends" with his iconic "How you doin'?" which became a universal icebreaker. Movies, too, have left their mark, with "fetch" from "Mean Girls" and "as if" from "Clueless" becoming part of our everyday chatter. And let's not forget the power of social media and internet culture, which has birthed terms like "selfie" and "hashtag," forever changing the way we communicate and share our lives with the world.

Slang isn't just a product of pop culture; it's also deeply rooted in regional and subcultural influences. In the UK, you might hear someone described as "cheeky" if they're being a bit impudent, or referred to as a "bloke" if they're just your average guy. Hop on over to Australia, and you'll quickly learn that "arvo" means afternoon, and everyone is your "mate." African American Vernacular English (AAVE) has gifted us with terms like "lit" for exciting events and "shade" for those subtle insults that cut to the bone. Meanwhile, skateboarding culture has its own lexicon, with "gnarly" capturing the essence of a challenging trick and "shred" describing the act of skateboarding with skill and flair. These regional and subcultural slangs enrich our language, adding layers of meaning and identity.

1. **FOMO (2004)** - Short for "Fear of Missing Out," expressing anxiety over missing fun or exciting events.
2. **Bougie (2000s)** - Short for bourgeois, used to describe something fancy or high-class, often with irony

3. **Glamping (2005)** - A portmanteau of "glamorous" and "camping," for luxury camping
4. **Bromance (2001)** - A close, non-romantic friendship between men
5. **Ghosting (2010s)** - When someone suddenly cuts off all communication without explanation.
6. **Dumpster Fire (2008)** - A chaotic or disastrous situation
7. **Big Oof (2010s)** - An expression for a significant mistake or setback
8. **Sus (Suspicious)** Something feels off or sketchy.
9. **Karen (Entitled or Demanding Person)** A pejorative term for a middle-aged woman acting entitled or demanding.
10. **Drip (Stylish or Cool Outfit)** Refers to stylish clothing or accessories.

As we look to the future, slang is poised to evolve at an even faster pace, thanks to technology and the internet. Global connectivity fosters cross-cultural exchanges, allowing slang to spread and morph across borders with unprecedented speed. Artificial intelligence and machine learning could play a role in creating or adopting new slang, as algorithms learn to mimic human communication styles. Changing social norms and cultural shifts will continue to influence slang usage, reflecting the values and priorities of each generation. It's exciting to imagine what new words will capture our collective imagination and become part of our daily lexicon.

Slang is a living testament to the creativity and adaptability of language. It reflects who we are, where we've been, and where we're going. So whether you're calling something "rad" or saying "cray," you're participating in a linguistic evolution that's as dynamic and diverse as the people who speak it.

14

Chapter 14: Mind-Boggling Coincidences

Have you ever experienced that spooky moment when you realize the universe might be playing some kind of cosmic joke on you? Like when you think about an old friend, and they suddenly call out of the blue, or when you hum a tune only to hear it blasting from a passing car? These coincidences often leave us scratching our heads, half-expecting Rod Serling to step out of the shadows and welcome us to "The Twilight Zone." But as it turns out, history—our old, dusty book of collective memory—is just as chock-full of these uncanny moments as our daily lives.

14.1 Historical Coincidences That Defy Explanation

Take the eerie parallels between Presidents Abraham Lincoln and John F. Kennedy. Both were elected to Congress in '46—1846 for Lincoln, 1946 for Kennedy. They stepped into the presidential shoes a century apart in 1860 and 1960, respectively. As if that wasn't enough to make you raise an eyebrow, both were assassinated on a fateful Friday while in the company of their wives. Lincoln met his tragic end in Ford's Theatre, while Kennedy was shot in a Lincoln car made by Ford. It's almost as if Ford had a vendetta against them. And then there's the sinister symmetry of their assassins: John Wilkes Booth and Lee Harvey Oswald. Both assassins met their demise before they could stand trial, adding another layer of intrigue to this historical coincidence. While some claim these parallels suggest reincarnation or some cosmic balancing act, others are quick to point out that many of these coincidences are more about clever storytelling than fact. The list of similarities has been exaggerated over the years, much like a fisherman's tale of the one that got away.

Another spine-tingling tale of coincidence involves the RMS Titanic and its fictional doppelgänger from Morgan Robertson's novella, "The Wreck of the Titan." Published in 1898, a full 14 years before the Titanic disaster, the book describes the fictional Titan as an "unsinkable" ship that meets its doom in the icy waters of the North Atlantic after colliding with an iceberg. Both Titan and Titanic share similar dimensions and capacities, with neither carrying enough lifeboats for their passengers. The real-life Titanic and Robertson's fictional vessel both sank in April, an eerily specific detail that has led some to speculate about the author's clairvoyance. However, Robertson attributed his prophetic writing to an understanding of maritime trends and shipbuilding, rather than an otherworldly insight. Still, the similarities are enough to make even the most skeptical among us pause.

The Battle of Waterloo is yet another historical event with an unexpected twist of fate, influenced by a volcanic eruption halfway across the world. In 1815, Mount Tambora in Indonesia erupted, spewing ash high into the atmosphere and causing climatic disturbances known as the "year without a summer." This led to a severe famine in Europe, weakening Napoleon's army with malnutrition and disease. When Napoleon met his final defeat at Waterloo, heavy rains—partly attributed to the volcanic eruption—turned the battlefield into a muddy quagmire, hampering his troops' movements and contributing to his downfall. It's as if Mother Nature decided to step in and play a hand in European history, proving that sometimes, the butterfly effect is more of a volcanic one.

Then we have the Curse of Tippecanoe, a pattern that claimed U.S. presidents elected in years ending in zero. It began with William Henry Harrison in 1840, and subsequent victims included Lincoln (1860), James A. Garfield (1880), William McKinley (1900), Warren G. Harding (1920), Franklin D. Roosevelt (1940), and Kennedy (1960). The curse seemed to break with Ronald Reagan, who survived an assassination attempt after being elected in 1980. Theories abound, ranging from Native American curses to mere statistical flukes. Whether you chalk it up to bad luck or historical happenstance, the Curse of Tippecanoe has left its mark on American presidential lore.

These historical coincidences remind us that the world is full of mysteries, not all of which can be explained by logic or reason.

They invite us to ponder the strange intersections of fate and history, where reality sometimes reads like a well-crafted novel, leaving us both intrigued and slightly bewildered.

14.2 Unbelievable Personal Stories of Coincidence

Imagine growing up thinking you're one of a kind, only to discover that your life is a mirror image of someone else's—right down to the name. That's precisely what happened to Jim Lewis and Jim Springer, identical twins separated at birth and raised 40 miles apart. Despite never having met, their lives unfolded as if scripted by a cosmic playwright with a penchant for the surreal. Both were named James by their adoptive families, setting the stage for a series of uncanny parallels. They each married women named Linda, only to divorce and remarry women named Betty. As if that weren't enough, both Jims had sons named James Allan (or Alan, depending on the whim of their respective birth certificates). Their similarities extended to careers in security, habits like chain-smoking, and even their choice of pet —a dog named Toy. It's as if fate, or some mischievous guardian angel, decided to make their lives a social experiment in synchronicity. Their eventual meeting at age 39 revealed these astonishing parallels, baffling psychologists and delighting conspiracy theorists everywhere.

The high seas, with their vastness and mystery, have long been the backdrop for tales of survival against all odds. But few stories are as bizarre as that of Hugh Williams, who managed to cheat death not once, but twice, separated by over a century. In 1660, a ship sank in the Menai Strait, leaving Hugh Williams as the sole survivor, clinging to a piece of wood amidst the wreckage. Fast forward to 1782, and history almost eerily repeated itself. Another ship, another fateful sinking in the same waters, and once again, a man named Hugh Williams emerged as the only survivor. He too was found holding onto a wooden fragment, as if the name itself were a life preserver. Whether it's coincidence, some kind of maritime magic, or just a really good swimming lesson passed down through generations, the tale of Hugh Williams stands as a testament to the quirks of fate.

There are stories that seem too wild to be true, and then there's the tale of Henry Ziegland, which reads like a plot twist from a Hollywood thriller. In 1893, Ziegland narrowly escaped death when his jilted lover's brother shot at him. The bullet grazed Ziegland's face and lodged itself into a tree, as if waiting for its moment to shine. Years later, in a twist of irony that would make even the most seasoned dramatist gasp, Ziegland decided to remove the tree using dynamite. The explosion dislodged the bullet, which struck and killed him on its belated journey. It's a tale that leaves you wondering if the bullet harbored a grudge or if it was simply a case of cosmic justice being served in the most spectacularly improbable fashion.

Then there's Joseph Figlock, a man who seemed to have a knack for being in the right place at the right time—or perhaps the wrong place, depending on how you look at it. In 1937, Figlock was walking down a street in Detroit when a baby fell from a high window, landing on him. Miraculously, both Figlock and the baby were unharmed, and the incident could have been chalked up as a one-off miracle. But fate had other plans. A year later, another baby took a nosedive from a window, landing on Figlock in a near-identical scenario. Once again, both emerged unscathed. It's almost as if Figlock had a gravitational pull for wayward infants or was a secret superhero with the power of baby-catching. These incidents not only made Figlock a local legend but also added a new dimension to the phrase "catching a break."

14.3 The Science Behind Coincidences

When you hear about coincidences, you might think the universe is conspiring to play tricks on us. However, there's often a logical explanation rooted in statistics and psychology. One such concept is the Law of Large Numbers, which suggests that with enough opportunities, even rare events become likely. Imagine yourself in a room filled with 23 people. You'd think the odds of two people sharing a birthday are slim, but statistical probability says otherwise. This is known as the birthday paradox, where there's a 50% chance two individuals will share the same birthday. It's like finding out you've been humming the same tune as your colleague—curious but not impossible. The more people you add to any scenario, the more likely odd coincidences will pop up, like when your neighbor's cat decides to mimic your morning yoga routine.

In the TV show *NCIS*, Special Agent Leroy Jethro Gibbs, played by Mark Harmon, has a series of rules he lives by and enforces with his team. Rule #39: "There is no such thing as a coincidence."

Speaking of routines, our brains love them. That's where pattern recognition comes into play. Our brains are wired to find connections in everything, whether they're real or not—a phenomenon known as apophenia. It's like that moment in childhood when you thought clouds were shaped like dragons or when every phone call from an unknown number seemed destined to be your long-lost relative. While this helped our ancestors avoid predators (because that rustle in the bushes might actually be a lion), it now leads us to see coincidences in random data. The brain's talent for connection can make you feel like you've won the cosmic lottery when you bump into an old friend in a foreign country. But, in reality, it's just your brain doing what it does best—making sense of the chaos.

Now, let's sprinkle in some selective memory and confirmation bias, where we like to remember the hits and forget the misses. Humans are notorious for recalling events that fit their beliefs and conveniently ignoring those that don't. It's why you might remember meeting three people with the same birthday as yours but forget the dozens who didn't. Your brain loves a good story and will often piece together fragments to create one. This is why conspiracy theories often feel so compelling; they weave together disparate facts into a narrative that feels coherent, even when it's more fiction than fact.

Probability has a starring role in all of this. It's the quiet force that explains why coincidences happen more often than we'd expect. Take lottery wins—those lucky few who win big. While it feels like an extraordinary stroke of fate, probability tells us that someone has to win. The odds are astronomically low, yet with millions of tickets sold, it's almost inevitable that someone will hit the jackpot. Or consider meeting someone with your name, which seems like a rare occurrence until you realize just how many people share common names. Probability lurks behind every surprising encounter and every peculiar event, serving as a reminder that while the universe might seem whimsical, it's actually playing by the rules.

Understanding the science behind coincidences doesn't make them any less magical. If anything, it adds a layer of appreciation for the intricacies of life. Recognizing the role of statistics, psychology, and probability in shaping these moments allows us to marvel at the world's complexity. While coincidences might be scientifically explainable, they still hold the power to surprise and delight us. And who doesn't love a good surprise? Now, as you ponder these odd occurrences, remember that the universe is vast, our brains are beautifully complex, and sometimes, things just happen.

Make a Difference with Your Review

Unlock the Power of Curiosity

"The mind is like a parachute—it works best when it's open."

— Frank Zappa

Thank you for diving into *Mind-Bending Trivia for Adults*! I hope you had as much fun reading it as I did putting it together. Trivia isn't just about facts—it's about sparking curiosity, making connections, and seeing the world in a whole new way.

If this book made you laugh, made you think, or gave you a story to share, I'd love to hear about it! Your review helps others discover the joy of mind-bending trivia and encourages me to keep unearthing more strange and surprising facts. Whether it's a quick note about your favorite part or a few words about why you enjoyed it, every review makes a difference.

Simply by leaving your honest opinion of this book on Amazon, you'll guide fellow trivia lovers to discover the information they're looking for and help them dive into the delightful world of quirky, unforgettable facts.

Sharing your thoughts is easy—just a few sentences can help others decide to jump into this trivia adventure. Thank you for being a part of this journey, and happy fact-finding!

https://is.gd/Mind_Bending

Scan QR Code
with your phone camera
to leave your review on Amazon.

Leave a review today!
Thanks,
Larry Solesbee

Conclusion

Well, dear reader, here we are at the finish line of our trivia-packed adventure. I hope you're not feeling as overwhelmed as a cat in a room full of rocking chairs. Because the very purpose of this book was to transform those everyday conversations into delightful exchanges, bursting with quirky facts and unexpected laughter. My mission was simple: to make you a walking, talking encyclopedia of fascinating tidbits that could turn any dull moment into a delightful exchange.

We've journeyed through a buffet of themed sections, each one a treasure chest of oddities and curiosities. From the technological wonders and futuristic musings in "Technology and the Future" to the bizarre realities of "History's Hidden Gems," we've explored it all. We dove into "Science Oddities" where the universe revealed its weirdest secrets. "Pop Culture and Modern Oddities" showed us just how peculiar our daily obsessions can be, while "Mind-Blowing Math and Numbers" made us scratch our heads in both confusion and awe.

Then there was "Nature's Mysteries," which unfolded the world's marvels and left us agog at the wonders of the natural world. "Laws and Customs You Won't Believe" had us questioning the sanity of our legal systems. We even dared to venture into the realm of "Time Travel and Sci-Fi Wonders," where the impossible seemed just a little bit more plausible.

Remember, the key takeaway from all these chapters is that trivia is not just about knowing obscure facts. It's about embracing curiosity, sparking conversation, and seeing the world from a fresh perspective. Whether it's recognizing the Fibonacci sequence in a sunflower or laughing about a law that prohibits suspicious salmon handling, these facts are here to enrich your life and conversations.

Now, I urge you to take this newfound wisdom and share it with the world. Be the person who lights up a room with an odd factoid or an unexpected story. Challenge your friends to trivia duels or bring these quirky nuggets to your next gathering. Spread the joy of learning and the thrill of discovery. Engage with others, and let the ripple effect of your knowledge inspire curiosity in those around you.

As we part ways, I want to thank you for choosing to embark on this journey with me. It's been a delight to guide you through these pages, and I hope you've had as much fun as I have had gathering all of these facts. Remember, trivia is not just a collection of facts, but a celebration of the wonder and whimsy of the world.

I'd love to hear from you about your experiences with the book. Did a particular fact tickle your fancy, or did you find yourself in a lively debate over one tidbit of trivia or another? Feel free to reach out, share your thoughts, and even suggest topics for future exploration. Your feedback is as valuable as a perfectly timed pun at a comedy club.

Before we close this chapter, let's have a quick index to help you navigate the treasure trove of knowledge we've unearthed:

Index

3D printing Ch 7.2
3D Printing Technology Ch 8.3
5G Wireless Networks Ch 3.3
55 Cancri e Ch 5.3
56 Kbps Modem Ch 3.3
300 Baud Modem Ch 3.3
1984 Ch 7.3
AAVE Ch 13.4
Abbasid Caliphate Ch 10.2
Abraham Lincoln Ch 4, Ch 14.1
absquatulate Ch 13
Abyss,The Ch 4.1, Ch 5
acacia honey Ch 2.1
Ada Lovelace Ch 10
Adams-Onís Treaty, The Ch 10.2
aeolipile Ch 10
aerial navigation Ch 11.3
African American Vernacular English
(AAVE) Ch 13.4
AGI Ch 8
aglet Ch 2.3, Ch 13.2
agraffe Ch 2.3, Ch 13.2
AI Ch 7.2, Ch 8
air conditioning Ch 10
Air Fryers Ch 8.3
Air Guitar World Championships Ch 6.1
Al Ain, UAE Ch 5.2
Alan Turing Ch 8
albatross Ch 3.1
Albert Einstein Ch 7.1
alchemy Ch 10.1
Alex Honnold Ch 3
Alex Mullen Ch 3
Alexa Ch 8
Alexander Fleming Ch 3.2
algorithms Ch 12.1
aluminum Ch 4.1
Amazon Rainforest Ch 5.3
Amazon Rainforest, The Ch 5.1
American Revolution Ch 10.1
Analytical Engine Ch 10
Andaman and Nicobar archipelago Ch
4.1
Anderson, Mary Ch 10
anglerfish Ch 9
Anglo-Zanzibar War Ch 10.2

animal noises Ch 1.2
animal welfare Ch 1
Antheil, George Ch 10
antifreeze proteins Ch 9
Aokigahara Ch 5.1
Apollo 1 fire disaster Ch 8.2
Apollo 11 Ch 3.2, Ch 8.2
Apollo 13 Ch 8.2
apophenia Ch 14.3
Arabs Ch 10.2
architecture Ch 12
Arctic fish Ch 9
Arctic tern Ch 3.1
Arizona Ch 5.2
armhole Ch 2.3, Ch 13.2
armscye Ch 2.3, Ch 13.2
Armstrong, Neil Ch 3.2, Ch 8.2
Arnold Schwarzenegger Ch 1.2
art of imitation, the Ch 9
Artemis program, NASA's Ch 8.2
Artificial General Intelligence (AGI) Ch 8
artificial intelligence Ch 3.3, Ch 7.2, Ch 8
artificial satellite Ch 8.2
artificially designed genomes Ch 9.2
Ashrita Furman Ch 3
Asimov, Isaac Ch 7.2
aspics Ch 2.2
asteroid mining Ch 8.2
astronauts Ch 3.2, Ch 5.3
astronomers Ch 9.1
Atanasoff-Berry Computer (ABC) Ch 10
Atanasoff, John Ch 10
Athena Ch 8
Atlantic Ocean Ch 3
Atlantic Ocean, South Ch 4.1
Atlantic, North Ch 14.1
Australia Ch 5.2, Ch 10.2, Ch 13.4
Austria Ch 6.1
automatic lubrication system Ch 10
autonomous vehicles Ch 8
avian espionage Ch 9
axions Ch 9.1
Ayrshire Ch 5.2
Aztecs Ch 2
Babbage, Charles Ch 10
Baby Jumping Festival Ch 6.1

Bach Ch 9.2
Back to the Future Ch 1.2
bacon Ch 2.1
Baghdad Ch 10.2
Bamboozled Ch 6.2, Ch 13.1
Bananas Ch 5.3
Bannock device Ch 2.3, Ch 13.2
basketball spinning Ch 1.3
Basque pelota Ch 11.3
Batesian mimicry Ch 9
Bats Ch 9
Battle of Cajamarca Ch 10.2
Battle of Talas Ch 10.2
Battle of Waterloo, The Ch 14.1
Bavaria Ch 10.1
Bedford County Ch 5.2
beer Ch 6.1
Beethoven Ch 9.2
Bell Ch 10
bell-bottoms Ch 13.4
bench pressing Ch 3
Benoît Lecomte Ch 3
Bermuda Triangle Ch 5.2
Bermuda Triangle of Transylvania Ch 5.1
Berners-Lee, Tim Ch 3.2
Bernhard Riemann Ch 12.1
Bernie Sanders' Mittens Ch 1.1
berries Ch 5.3
Big Brother Ch 7.3
Big Oof Ch 10.3, Ch 13.4
bikinis Ch 6
Bilderberg Group, the Ch 10.1
billiards Ch 11.2
binary arithmetic Ch 10
binge-watching Ch 7.3
bingo Ch 11.2
binomial coefficients Ch 12
Biodegradable Plastics Ch 8.3
biological antifreeze Ch 9
bioluminescence Ch 5
bioluminescent Ch 5.2
bioluminescent creatures Ch 5
bioluminescent fungi Ch 5
bioluminescent markers Ch 5
biotechnology Ch 9.2
birthday paradox, the Ch 14.3

Bjornsson, Hafthor Ch 3
black & white TV Ch 8.2
Black Forest in Germany Ch 5.1
Black Hills Forest Ch 5.1
black holes Ch 7.1
black marlin Ch 3.1
Black Mountain, Queensland Ch 5.2
Black Widow Ch 1.2
Blair Witch Ch 5.1
bling Ch 3.4
Blockchain Technology Ch 8.3
Bloemfontein Ch 4
bloke Ch 13.4
bloviate Ch 13
Blue Origin Ch 8.2
blueprint of life Ch 9.2, Ch 12.2
Bluetooth Headphones Ch 8.3
Bluetooth Technology Ch 8.3
Blunt, Emily Ch 1.2
Bohemian Club Ch 10.1
Bolivia Ch 6.1
Bonus Army March, The Ch 10.2
Booth, John Wilkes Ch 14.1
bootstrap paradox Ch 7.1
Bougie Ch 10.3, Ch 13.4
box tent Ch 2.3, Ch 13.2
Bradbury, Ray Ch 7.3
Braga Ch 5.2
Poland Ch 5.2
Brazil Ch 10.2
break dancing Ch 11.3
Britain Ch 5.3, Ch 10.2
British Empire Ch 10.2
broken pianos Ch 1
Bromance Ch 10.3, Ch 13.4
Brown Mountain Ch 5.1
bulletin boards Ch 3.2
bulletproof helmets Ch 10
bulletproof vests Ch 10
bumfuzzle Ch 13
Buñol, Spain Ch 6.1
Burger King Ch 2
Burj Khalifa Ch 3.3
cacao beans Ch 2
calcite concretions Ch 5.2
Camcorders Ch 8.3

Camera Phones Ch 8.3
Cameron, James Ch 1.2
Canada Ch 4, Ch 4.1, Ch 5.2, Ch 11.2
Canasta Ch 11.2
Canoe slalom Ch 11.3
Canoodle Ch 6.2, Ch 13.1
Cape Town Ch 4
Captain Kirk Ch 7.2
car wash Ch 6
carbon filament Ch 10
Caribbean Ch 10.2
carpool Ch 6
Carrier, Willis Ch 10
Carrom Ch 11.2
cat behavior Ch 9.2
Cat Ch 3.1
Cave of Crystals Ch 5.2
CDMS Ch 9.1
Celine Dion Ch 1.2
censorship Ch 7.3
Central America Ch 5.1
cephalopods Ch 9
Cesena Ch 5.2
Challenger disaster Ch 8.2
chameleons Ch 5.1
champagne Ch 2.3, Ch 13.2
chaos theory Ch 12.2
Charles Babbage Ch 10
cheeky Ch 13.4
cheese Ch 2.1
Cheese Rolling festival Ch 6.1
cheetah Ch 3.1
chemical reaction Ch 5
chess Ch 11.2
chewing gum Ch 6
Chicago's deep-dish pizza Ch 2
Chihuahua Ch 3.1
chili Ch 2.1
China Ch 10.2
chocolate bar Ch 2
chocolate Ch 2, Ch 4
Chocolate Hills Ch 5.2
Christopher Nolan Ch 1.2
chromatophores Ch 9
chthonic Ch 13
Chutes and Ladders Ch 11.2

cloning Ch 1.2
closed timelike curves (CTCs) Ch 7.1
cloud forests Ch 5.1
Clownfish Ch 9
CN Tower, the Ch 12.2
Cochrane, Josephine Ch 10
Codswallop Ch 6.2, Ch 13.1
Cold War Ch 8.2
Collatz Conjecture Ch 12.1
collywobbles Ch 13
Columbia disaster Ch 8.2
columella nas Ch 2.3, Ch 13.2
comet's tail Ch 5.3
communicator Ch 7.2
compass Ch 10.1
computer algorithms Ch 12
computer programmer Ch 10
computer virus Ch 5.3
Contact Lenses, Disposable Ch 8.3
contemporary experimentation Ch 9.2
Cooper, Martin Ch 7.2
Cooper's Hill in Gloucestershire Ch 6.1
cornflakes Ch 2.2
Corrective Optics Space Telescope Axial
Replacement (COSTAR) Ch 3.2
cosmic breadcrumbs Ch 9.1
cosmic bumper cars Ch 9.2
cosmic demolition derby Ch 9.1
cosmic exploration Ch 8.2
cosmic glue Ch 9.1
cosmic joyride Ch 8.2
cosmic merry-go-round Ch 9.1
cosmic microwave background radiation
Ch 9.1
cosmic strings Ch 7.1
cosmos, the Ch 12.2
COSTAR Ch 3.2
cowrie shells Ch 11.2
Cows Ch 5.3
crafting meat Ch 2.2
crapulence Ch 2.3, Ch 13.2
cray Ch 13.4
Crichton, Michael Ch 1.2
CRISPR technology Ch 9.2
Crokinole Ch 11.2
Crows Ch 3.1

Cryogenic Dark Matter Search (CDMS) Ch 9.1
cryptic patterning Ch 9
cryptobiosis Ch 9
cryptographer Ch 13
cryptography Ch 8, Ch 12.1
cuckoo bird Ch 9
cumulative weight Ch 3
Curiosity Ch 3.2, Ch 8.2
Curse of Tippecanoe, the Ch 14.1
cyber warfare Ch 7.3
cyberpunk Ch 7.3
cybersecurity Ch 7.3
cylinder Ch 4.1
D'oh! Ch 13.4
da Vinci, Leonardo Ch 12.2
Dalibor Jablanovic Ch 3
Daniel Peter Ch 2
Dark Matter Ch 9.1
Darth Vader Ch 1.2
Dartmouth Summer Research Project Ch 8
Data Transfer Ch 3.3
David Prowse Ch 1.2
Day of the Dead Ch 6.1
deadlifting Ch 3
Dean Karnazes Ch 3
Death Valley Ch 5.2
deck of cards Ch 3
Declaration of Sentiments Ch 10.2
Deep Blue Ch 8
Deep-sea anglerfish Ch 5
deepest oceanic point Ch 4.1
Defenestration Ch 13
DeLorean Ch 1.2, Ch 10
dial-up modems Ch 3.2
DiCaprio, Leonardo Ch 1.2
dice Ch 11.2
Digital Assistants Ch 8.3
Digital Cameras Ch 8.3
digital computers Ch 10
digital pickpockets Ch 8
digital subterfuge Ch 7.3
Digital Video Recorders (DVRs) Ch 8.3
dillydallying Ch 13
Dingleberry Ch 6.2, Ch 13.1

dinoflagellates Ch 5
Dion, Celine Ch 1.2
disappearing lakes Ch 4.1
Discombobulated Ch 6.2, Ch 13.1
dishwasher Ch 10
Disposable Contact Lenses Ch 8.3
DNA Ancestry Kits Ch 8.3
DNA Ch 9.2, Ch 12.2
DNA Fingerprinting Ch 8.3
Doe, Roland Ch 1.2
Dogs Ch 9, Ch 9.2
dolphin communication Ch 9.2
dolphin, pink river Ch 5.1
Dolphins Ch 3.1, Ch 5.3, Ch 9, Ch 9.2
Door Locks, Smart Ch 8.3
Door to Hell Ch 5.2
dope Ch 13.4
double-slit experiment Ch 9.2
Dragon's Blood Tree Ch 4.1
dragonfly Ch 3.1
Drip Ch 10.3, Ch 13.4
Drone racing Ch 11.3
duct tape Ch 7.3, Ch 8.2
dumbbells Ch 3
Dumpster Fire Ch 10.3, Ch 13.4
dung beetle Ch 3.1
DVDs Ch 8.3
DVRs Ch 8.3
dwarf planet Ch 5.3
dysania Ch 2.3, Ch 13.2
dystopian future Ch 8
E-sports Ch 11.3
E.T. the Extra-Terrestrial Ch 1.2
Eamonn Keane Ch 3
Earl Grey tea Ch 7.2
East Asia Ch 11.2
echolocation Ch 9
Ecuador Ch 4.1
Edison Ch 10
eel baskets Ch 5.2
Egypt Ch 11.2
Egyptian tombs Ch 5.3
Eiffel Tower Ch 4, Ch 5.3
Eiffel, Gustave Ch 4
Einstein, Albert Ch 7.1
El Capitan Ch 3

El Colacho Ch 6.1
Electric Bicycles Ch 8.3
electric light bulb Ch 10
Electric Scooters Ch 8.3
Electric Toothbrushes Ch 8.3
electronic switching Ch 10
electroreceptors Ch 9
elephants Ch 3.1
Elijah McCoy Ch 10
Elizabeth Cady Stanton Ch 10.2
Eloi Ch 7.3
Emily Blunt Ch 1.2
Emu War, the Ch 10.2
Endeavour Ch 3.2
England Ch 6.1
England's Peak District Ch 11.1
Epitome Ch 13
Ermal Fraze Ch 4.1
esoteric Christianity Ch 10.1
ESPN Ch 11.1
ethical questions Ch 9.2
etymology Ch 13
Eukonkanto Ch 6.1
Europe Ch 10.2, Ch 14.1
Europeans Ch 2
Everest Base Camp Ch 11.1
exclamation mark Ch 2.3, Ch 13.2
exoplanet Ch 5.3
Exorcist, The Ch 1.2
Exploding Kittens Ch 11.2
Extremadura Ch 6.1
Extreme Ironing World Championships
Ch 11.1
eye and pyramid Ch 10.1
eyebrows Ch 2.3, Ch 5.3, Ch 13.2
Face Masks, Reusable Ch 8.3
Fahrenheit 451 Ch 7.3
fake news Ch 7.3
Falcon Heavy launch Ch 8.2
Feliks Zemdegs Ch 3
feline Ch 9.2
Fermi Gamma-ray Space Telescope Ch
9.1
fetch Ch 13.4
Fiber Optic Internet Ch 3.3
Fibonacci sequence Ch 12, Ch 12.2

Fibonacci spiral Ch 12
Figlock, Joseph Ch 14.2
final frontier, the Ch 8.2
Finland Ch 6.1
Finn McCool Ch 5.2
fireflies Ch 5
firemen torch literature Ch 7.3
Flabbergasted Ch 6.2, Ch 13.1
flamboyance Ch 5.3
flamingo tongues Ch 2.2
flamingos Ch 5.3
flatbread Ch 2
flatfish Ch 9
Fleming, Alexander Ch 3.2
Flibbertigibbet Ch 6.2, Ch 13.1
flightless birds Ch 10.2
Florida Ch 10.2
flower power Ch 13.4
fluid dynamics Ch 12.1
Flummox Ch 13
fluorescence Ch 5
Foldable Smartphones Ch 8.3
FOMO Ch 10.3, Ch 13.4
food printing Ch 7.2
Ford, Harrison Ch 1.2
Ford's Theatre Ch 14.1
fourth dimension Ch 7.3
foxfire fungus Ch 5
fractal geometry Ch 12.2
France Ch 11.2, Ch 11.3
Francisco Pizarro Ch 10.2
Franklin D. Roosevelt Ch 14.1
Franklin Township Ch 5.2
Free solo climbing Ch 3
Freemasons Ch 10.1
frequency-hopping spread spectrum
technology Ch 10
Fry, Joseph Ch 2
galaxies Ch 12.2
galaxy rotation curves Ch 9.1
game of little horses Ch 11.2
gamma rays Ch 9.1
Gansu Province, China   Ch 5.2
garden gnomes Ch 1.3
Garfield, James A. Ch 14.1
gastronomy Ch 2.2

gelatin molds Ch 2.2
Gene editing Ch 9.2
general theory of relativity Ch 7.1
genetic disorders Ch 9.2
genetic engineering Ch 1.2
genetic therapy Ch 3.2
genomes Ch 9.2
Geographical Oddities Ch 4.1
Geography Ch 5.2
Geology Ch 5.2
George Antheil Ch 10
George Orwell Ch 7.3
Germany Ch 5.1, Ch 11.1, Ch 11.2
gezelligheid Ch 13.3
Ghosting Ch 10.3, Ch 13.4
giant marbles Ch 5.2
Giant pandas Ch 5.3
Giant's Causeway Ch 5.2
Gibraltar Ch 4
Gibson, William Ch 7.3
Gigabit Connections Ch 3.3
gigil Ch 13.3
Giraffes Ch 5.3
glabella Ch 2.3, Ch 13.2
Glamping Ch 10.3, Ch 13.4
Glasses, Smart Ch 8.3
gliding Ch 11.3
Gloom Ch 11.2
glow sticks Ch 5
glow-in-the-dark products Ch 5
glowing jellyfish Ch 5
glowing millipedes Ch 5
glowing orbs Ch 5.1
glowworms Ch 5.2
gluttony Ch 2.2
gnarly Ch 13.4
Go Ch 11.2
Goat cheese Ch 2.1
gobbledygook Ch 13
God particle Ch 9.2
Godfather, The Ch 1.2
Golden Ratio, the Ch 12, Ch 12.2
goldfish Ch 6
gorilla Ch 6
Gouda Ch 6.1
GPS Ch 4.1

GPS for Public Use Ch 8.3
graham crackers Ch 2.2
grandfather paradox, The Ch 7.1
gravitational effects Ch 9.1
gravitational lensing Ch 9.1
gravitational pull Ch 7.1
gravity Ch 3, Ch 4.1, Ch 9.1
Great Dane Ch 3.1
Great Depression, the Ch 2.1, Ch 10.2
Great Wall of China Ch 4
grey-headed albatross Ch 3.1
Griffith Park Ch 5.2
griffonage Ch 2.3, Ch 13.2
groovy Ch 13.4
ground beef Ch 2
guinea pigs Intro, Ch 1, Ch 6
Gustave Eiffel Ch 4
H.G. Wells Ch 7.3
habitats Ch 7.2
Hafthor Bjornsson Ch 3
Hall of Records Ch 4
Hamburg, Germany Ch 2
hamburger Ch 2
Hansel and Gretel Ch 5.1
Harding, Warren G. Ch 14.1
Harmon, Mark Ch 14.3
harpy eagle Ch 3.1
Harrison Ford Ch 1.2
Harrison, William Henry Ch 14.1
hashtag Ch 13.4
health foods Ch 2.2
healthcare Ch 8
heart of a shrimp Ch 5
Hedy Lamarr Ch 10
hemolymph Ch 5
Henry Ziegland Ch 14.2
Here's Johnny Ch 1.2
hermaphroditism Ch 9
Heron of Alexandria Ch 10
hexagonal carpet Ch 1.2
hide and seek Ch 9.2
Higgs boson Ch 9.2
highest capital city Ch 4
Himalayan range Ch 4.1
Hip-hop culture Ch 13.4
Hnefatafl Ch 11.2

Hollis Cantrell Ch 3
holodeck Ch 7.2
Home Security Cameras Ch 8.3
honey Ch 2.1, Ch 5.3
honey, acacia Ch 2.1
Honnold, Alex Ch 3
Hoya-Baciu Forest Ch 5.1
Hubble Space Telescope Ch 3.2, Ch 8.2
Hugh Williams Ch 14.2
Human Genome Project Ch 3.2
human tissue Ch 7.2
humanoid robots Ch 7.2
hurricanes Ch 12.2
Hybrid Cars Ch 8.3
I'll be back Ch 1.2
IBM's Deep Blue Ch 8
ice cream Ch 2
iceberg Ch 14.1
Iceland Ch 6.1
Illuminati Ch 10.1
imitation Ch 9
Inca Empire Ch 10.2
Incan Emperor Atahualpa Ch 10.2
Inception Ch 1.2
India Ch 4.1, Ch 5.1, Ch 5.2, Ch 11.2
Indian Ocean Ch 4.1
Indiana Jones Ch 1.2
Indonesia Ch 13.3, Ch 14.1
Industrial Revolution Ch 10.2
information superhighway Ch 3.2
infrared Ch 8.2
Instagram filter Ch 12
International Space Station (ISS) Ch 8.2
internet Ch 3.2
internet meme Ch 1.1
interrobang Ch 2.3, Ch 13.2
iPods Ch 8.3
Ireland, Northern Ch 5.2
Irish giant Finn McCool Ch 5.2
iron (electric or battery-operated Ch 11.1
ironing board Ch 11.1
Isaac Asimov Ch 7.2
Ivan Pavlov Ch 9.2
Jablanovic, Dalibor Ch 3
jaguar Ch 5.1
James A. Garfield Ch 14.1

James Cameron Ch 1.2
James Earl Jones Ch 1.2
James Webb Space Telescope Ch 8.2
Japan Ch 5.1, Ch 5.3, Ch 6, Ch 6.1
jayus Ch 13.3
Jebel Hafeet Ch 5.2
jeu des petits chevaux Ch 11.2
Jim Lewis Ch 14.2
Jim Springer Ch 14.2
Johansson, Scarlett Ch 1.2
John Atanasoff Ch 10
John F. Kennedy Ch 14.1
John Lilly Ch 9.2
John McCarthy Ch 8
John Wilkes Booth Ch 14.1
Jonas Salk Ch 3.2
Jonathan the tortoise Ch 3.1
Jones, James Earl Ch 1.2
Joseph Figlock Ch 14.2
Joseph Fry Ch 2
Josephine Cochrane Ch 10
Julius Maddox Ch 3
Jurassic Park Ch 1.2
kangaroo Ch 6
karaoke Ch 7.1
Karen Ch 10.3, Ch 13.4
Karnazes, Dean Ch 3
Karpacz Ch 5.2
Kate Winslet Ch 1.2
Keanu Reeves Ch 1.2
Kearney, Michael Ch 3
Kennedy, John F. Ch 14.1
Kerfuffle Ch 6.2, Ch 13.1
Kevlar Ch 10
Khasi Ch 5.1
Knight, Margaret Ch 10
Koalas Ch 5.3
Kobold Ch 5.1
Koekohe Beach Ch 5.2
komorebi Ch 13.3
korfball Ch 11.3
Krampusnacht Ch 6.1
Kurzweil, Ray Ch 8
Kwolek, Stephanie Ch 10
La Paz, Bolivia Ch 4
La Tomatina Ch 6.1

lackadaisical Ch 13
Ladakh, India Ch 4.1, Ch 5.2
Lamarr, Hedy Ch 10
lancet liver fluke Ch 9
Lanzhou Ch 5.2
Large Hadron Collider, The Ch 9.1, Ch 9.2
largest pizza Ch 2
Last Supper, The Ch 12.2
Latimer, Lewis Ch 10
Latin America Ch 10.2
Laughter is the best medicine Ch 9.2
Law of Large Numbers Ch 14.3
lawnmower Ch 3
leaf-tailed gecko Ch 9
LED Light Bulbs Ch 8.3
Lee Harvey Oswald Ch 14.1
Leicester Ch 11.1
Lemurs Ch 5.1
Leonardo da Vinci Ch 12.2
Leonardo DiCaprio Ch 1.2
Leonardo of Pisa Ch 12
Lesotho Ch 4
Lewis Latimer Ch 10
Lewis, Jim Ch 14.2
Liber Abaci Ch 12
Liechtenstein Ch 4
Lilly, John Ch 9.2
limestone pillars Ch 5.2
Lincoln, Abraham Ch 4, Ch 14.1
Lion King, The Ch 1.2
lionfish Ch 9
lit Ch 13.4
live pigeon shooting Ch 11.3
lollygagging Ch 13
longest border Ch 4
longest continuous kiss Ch 1.3
Los Angeles Ch 5.2
Lost Lake, Oregon's Ch 4.1
Loteria Ch 11.2
Lovelace, Ada Ch 10
luciferase Ch 5
Luddites, The Ch 10.2
Ludo Ch 11.2
lungs of the Earth, the Ch 5.1
M&M's Ch 1.2
machine learning algorithms Ch 3.3

machine learning Ch 8
Madagascar Ch 5.1
Maddox, Julius Ch 3
magic Ch 10.1
magnetic hill phenomenon Ch 5.2
magnetic hills Ch 4.1
magnetite Ch 9
Maharashtra, India Ch 5.2
Malarky Ch 6.2, Ch 13.1
Maldives Ch 6
mamihlapinatapai Ch 13.3
manned missions to Mars Ch 8.2
mantis shrimp Ch 9
maple syrup Ch 2.1
maple-glazed donuts Ch 2.1
marathon Ch 3
Margaret Knight Ch 10
margarine Ch 2.2, Ch 6
Mariana Trench Ch 4.1
Mark Harmon Ch 14.3
marlin Ch 3.1
Mars Ch 7.2
Mars Rover Ch 3.2
Mars Rover missions, NASA's Ch 8.2
marsupial Ch 6
Martian colonies Ch 3.2
martian mojito Ch 8.2
Martian terrain Ch 3.2
Martin Cooper Ch 7.2
Marvin Minsky Ch 8
Mary Anderson Ch 10
Maryland Ch 5.1
masters of disguise Ch 9
mate Ch 13.4
Matrix Ch 7.3
Matrix, The Ch 1.2
Maya Ch 2
mayonnaise Ch 2.1
McCarthy, John Ch 8
McCool, Finn Ch 5.2
McCoyElijah Ch 10
McDonald's Ch 2
McKinley, William Ch 14.1
meatless diet Ch 2.2
medicine Ch 9.2
medieval banquet Ch 2.2

Medieval feasts Ch 2.2
meme Ch 1, Ch 1.1
Men in Black Ch 1.2
Menai Strait Ch 14.2
Mensch ärgere Dich nicht Ch 11.2
Mesoamericans Ch 2.1
Mesopotamia Ch 11.2
Metabo Law Ch 6
methane hydrates Ch 5.2
Mexican soldiers Ch 10.2
Mexico Ch 5.2, Ch 6.1, Ch 11.2
Mice and Mystics Ch 11.2
Michael Crichton Ch 1.2
Michael Kearney Ch 3
micro-nations Ch 4
microscopic plankton Ch 5
microwave oven Ch 10
Migratory birds Ch 9
milk chocolate Ch 2
milky seas Ch 5
Milky Way galaxy Ch 5.3
Millau Viaduct Ch 3.3
Milly the Chihuahua Ch 3.1
mimic octopus Ch 9
mimicry Ch 9
minimus Ch 2.3, Ch 13.2
Minsky, Marvin Ch 8
mobile phone Ch 7.2
mock apple pie Ch 2.2
modems Ch 3.2, Ch 3.3
Modified Newtonian Dynamics (MOND) Ch 9.1
Moeraki Boulder Ch 5.2
molecular scalpel Ch 9.2
Mona Lisa Ch 5.3
Monaco Ch 4
monarch butterfly Ch 9
Moncton Ch 4.1
MOND Ch 9.1
Monkey Buffet Festival Ch 6.1
Monopoly Ch 11.2
moonwalks Ch 8.2
Morgan Robertson Ch 14.1
Morlocks Ch 7.3
Motorola Ch 7.2
Mount Chimborazo in Ecuador Ch 4.1

Mount Everest Ch 4.1
Mount Rushmore Ch 4
Mount Tambora Ch 14.1
mouthwash Ch 5.3
MRI Machines Ch 8.3
Mullen, Alex Ch 3
Muslim world Ch 10.2
My Heart Will Go On Ch 1.2
Mystery Spot in Griffith Park Ch 5.2
Naica Mine Ch 5.2
nail clippings Ch 1.3
Namsan Park, South Korea Ch 5.2
Napoleon's army Ch 14.1
NASA's Artemis program Ch 8.2
NASA's Mars Rover missions Ch 8.2
Native American curses Ch 14.1
Nauru Ch 4
nautilus shell Ch 12
Navajo sandstone Ch 5.2
Navier-Stokes Existence and Smoothness problem, The Ch 12.1
Navy, U.S. Ch 10
NCIS Ch 14.3
Neil Armstrong Ch 3.2, Ch 8.2
Neo Ch 1.2, Ch 7.3
Netflix Ch 1, Ch 8
neural networks Ch 8
Neuralink brain implant chip Ch 3.2
Neuromancer Ch 7.3
New Brunswick Ch 5.2
New Jersey Ch 5.2
New York-style pizza Ch 2
New Zealand Ch 5.2
NFTs Ch 8.3
Nguni Bantu Ch 13.3
Nikola Tesla Ch 9.2, Ch 10
Nincompoop Ch 6.2, Ch 13.1
Nolan, Christopher Ch 1.2
North Atlantic Ch 14.1
North Carolina Ch 5.1
North Sentinel Island Ch 4.1
Northern Ireland Ch 5.2
nostrils Ch 2.3, Ch 13.2
Novikov self-consistency principle Ch 7.1
obesity Ch 6
octopus Ch 3.1, Ch 5.3, Ch 9

Olmecs Ch 2
Olympic Events Ch 11.3
Olympic Games Ch 11.3
Olympics, Paris Ch 11.3
one-dimensional loops Ch 7.1
Orroroo, South Australia Ch 5.2
optical illusion Ch 4.1
Oregon's Lost Lake Ch 4.1
organ transplant Ch 3.2
organized crime Ch 1.2
Orkney Islands Ch 5.3
Orwell, George Ch 7.3
Oswald, Lee Harvey Ch 14.1
overmorrow Ch 2.3, Ch 13.2
P vs NP Problem Ch 12.1
Pac-Man Ch 11.3
Pachisi Ch 11.2
Pacific Ch 3
Pacific Northwest Ch 10.2
Panama Canal Ch 3.3
pancake Ch 2.1
paper bag machine Ch 10
paper mills Ch 10.2
paper-making technology Ch 10.2
paradoxes Ch 7.1
parallel polymer chains Ch 10
parasitic worm Ch 9
Parcheesi Ch 11.2
Paria Canyon-Vermilion Cliffs Ch 5.2
Paris Olympics Ch 11.3
Park Place Ch 11.2
Parker Solar Probe Ch 8.2
Parkour Ch 11.3
Parthenon in Athens Ch 12, Ch 12.2
Pascal's Triangle Ch 12
Pastry War, The Ch 10.2
Pavlov, Ivan Ch 9.2
Pavlov's dogs Ch 9.2
Pavlovian Ch 9.2
PCP Ch 1.2
Peace of Westphalia, The Ch 10.2
peanut butter Ch 2.1
pena ajena Ch 13.3
penicillin Ch 3.2
Pennsylvania Ch 5.2
Perseverance Ch 3.2, Ch 8.2

Persnickety Ch 6.2, Ch 13.1
Personal Computers Ch 8.3
personalized medicine Ch 3.2
Peter, Daniel Ch 2
petrichor Ch 2.3, Ch 13.2
PhD Ch 3
phi, φ Ch 12.2
Phil Shaw Ch 11.1
Philippines Ch 5.2
phobias Ch 7.2
phosphenes Ch 2.3, Ch 13.2
photogenic Ch 12.2
pi Ch 3
pickle Ch 2.1
Pig War, The Ch 10.2
pineapples Ch 2.2, Ch 5.3, Ch 12
Pinecones Ch 12
pink river dolphin Ch 5.1
Pinnacles Desert Ch 5.2
Pinochle Ch 11.2
Pizarro, Francisco Ch 10.2
pizza Ch 2
pizza, largest Ch 2
platypus Ch 9
playlist Ch 8
Plugs, Smart Ch 8.3
Plunge for Distance Ch 11.3
Pluto Ch 5.3
pneumonoultramicroscopicsilicovolcanoc
oniosis Ch 13
pogs Ch 13
polio Ch 3.2
Poltergeist Ch 1.2
polybenzamide Ch 10
polymer chemistry Ch 10
pomegranates Ch 12
pop-top can Ch 4.1
Poppycock Ch 6.2, Ch 13.1
Portable Solar Chargers Ch 8.3
Portugal Ch 5.2, Ch 10.2
Post-it Notes Ch 8.3
powdered eggs Ch 2.2
Pretoria Ch 4
prime numbers Ch 12.1
Probability Ch 14.3
prongs Ch 2.3, Ch 13.2

prosthetics Ch 7.2
prototyping Ch 7.2
Prowse, David Ch 1.2
psychology Ch 14.3
pull-tab Ch 4.1
Pumpernickel Ch 6.2, Ch 13.1
quadriplegics Ch 3.2
quahog clam Ch 5.3
quantum mechanics Ch 7.1
quantum physics Ch 9.2
quantum tunneling Ch 7.1
question mark Ch 2.3, Ch 13.2
quetzal Ch 5.1
quomodocunquize Ch 13
rabbit populations Ch 12
Racetrack Playa Ch 5.2
rad Ch 13.4
radiation exposure Ch 10
railway industry Ch 10
rainforests Ch 5.1
rationing Ch 2.2
ravens Ch 3.1
Ray Bradbury Ch 7.3
Ray Kurzweil Ch 8
Reagan, Ronald Ch 14.1
Real McCoy, The Ch 10
Red Planet Ch 3.2
Reese's Pieces Ch 1.2
Reeves, Keanu Ch 1.2
Reforestation Ch 5.1
refrigerator Ch 1.2
replicators Ch 7.2
Reusable Face Masks Ch 8.3
reusable rockets Ch 8.2
Reusable Water Bottles Ch 8.3
Reynolds Metals Company Ch 4.1
Rhythmic gymnastics Ch 11.3
Ride-sharing Apps Ch 8.3
Riemann Hypothesis Ch 12.1
Riemann, Bernhard Ch 12.1
ring pull mechanism Ch 4.1
Ritz crackers Ch 2.2
Riz Ch 13.4
RMS Titanic Ch 14.1
roasted soybeans Ch 6.1
Robert Wadlow Ch 3

Robertson, Morgan Ch 14.1
robotic pioneers Ch 8.2
robotics Ch 7.2
rockets, reusable Ch 8.2
rogue waves Ch 5.2
Roland Doe Ch 1.2
Romagna, Italy Ch 5.2
Romania Ch 5.1
Rome Ch 5.3
Ronald Reagan Ch 14.1
Roosevelt, Franklin D. Ch 14.1
rose-cross symbol Ch 10.1
Rosicrucians, The Ch 10.1
Royal Game of Ur, The Ch 11.2
rubber ducks Ch 1.3
Rubik's Cube Ch 3
Rule #39 Ch 14.3
rumbling Ch 2.3, Ch 13.2
Russian Roulette Ch 11.2
sacred groves Ch 5.1
sailing stones Ch 5.2
Salk, Jonas Ch 3.2
salmon Ch 6
Salt Lake City Ch 5.2
Salvador Dalí Ch 5.2
Sanath Bandara Ch 3
Saturn Ch 5.3
saudade Ch 13.3
Scarlett Johansson Ch 1.2
schadenfreude Ch 11.2, Ch 13.3
Schwarzenegger, Arnold Ch 1.2
Sci-Fi Technologies Ch 7.2
scientific creativity Ch 9.2
Scotland, UK Ch 5.2, Ch 5.3
Sea of Trees Ch 5.1
sea snakes Ch 9
Sebastian Shaw Ch 1.2
secret handshakes Ch 10.1
Secret Hitler Ch 11.2
secret societies Ch 10.1
self-driving cars Ch 3.3, Ch 8.1, Ch 8.3
selfie Ch 13.4
Selfie Sticks Ch 8.3
Selleck, Tom Ch 1.2
Seneca Falls Convention, The Ch 10.2
Senet Ch 11.2

Sentinelese Ch 4.1
Setsubun Ch 6.1
Settlers of Catan Ch 11.2
shade Ch 13.4
Shah Jahan Ch 4
Sharks Ch 5.3
Shaw, Phil Ch 11.1
Shaw, Sebastian Ch 1.2
Shenanigans Ch 6.2, Ch 13.1
Sherlocks Ch 3.1
shirtless Ch 6
shoelaces Ch 2.3, Ch 13.2
shortest international border Ch 4
shred Ch 13.4
Simpsons, The Ch 13.4
Siri Ch 8
skateboard trick Ch 13.4
skateboarding Ch 11.3
Skedaddle Ch 6.2, Ch 13.1
skeletons Ch 1.2
ski ballet Ch 11.3
sleeping bear Ch 6
sleeves Ch 2.3, Ch 13.2
Sloths Ch 5.3
Smart Door Locks Ch 8.3
Smart Glasses Ch 8.3
Smart Plugs Ch 8.3
Smart Speakers Ch 8, Ch8.3
Smart Thermostats Ch 8.3
smartphone Ch 3.2, Ch 7.3
Smartwatches Ch 8.3
Smith, Will Ch 1.2
snowflake Ch 5.3
social creatures Ch 1
social media Ch 7.3
social media manipulation Ch 7.3
socks Ch 7.1
Socotra Ch 4.1
soda can Ch 4.1
Solar panels Ch 3.3
solar winds Ch 8.2
solo synchronized swimming Ch 11.3
Son Doong Cave Ch 5.2
sonar Ch 9
Sorry Ch 11.2
South Africa Ch 4

South Africa, Harrismith, Free State
Province Ch 5.2
South Atlantic Ocean Ch 4.1
Soviet Union Ch 8.2
space colonization Ch 8.2
space habitats Ch 8.2
space race Ch 8.2
space shuttle Ch 8.2
Space Shuttle Endeavour Ch 3.2
Space tourism Ch 8.2
spacewalks Ch 3.2
SpaceX Ch 8.2
Spain Ch 4, Ch 6.1, Ch 10.2, Ch 11.2, Ch
11.3
Spanish Ch 13.3
Spanish conquistadors Ch 10.2
Spanish dominance in South America Ch
10.2
Spanish explorers Ch 2
Speakers, Smart Ch 8, Ch8.3
Spices Ch 2.2
spiral staircases Ch 12
spoons Ch 3
Springer, Jim Ch 14.2
Sputnik Ch 8.2
square Ch 10.1
square hamburger Ch 2
stalagmites Ch 5.2
Stanford prison experiment Ch 9.2
Stanford University Ch 9.2
Stanton, Elizabeth Cady Ch 10.2
Star Trek Ch 7.2
Star Trek: The Next Generation Ch 7.2
Star Wars" memorabilia Ch 1.3
statistics Ch 14.3
stay-on-tab Ch 4.1
steam engine Ch 10
Stephanie Kwolek Ch 10
sterile neutrinos Ch 9.1
strawberries Ch 5.3
Streaming Devices Ch 8.3
Streaming Services Ch 8.3
strong hydrogen bonds Ch 10
stuffed dormice Ch 2.2
submarine Ch 4.1
sugar sculptures Ch 2.2

Sultan of Zanzibar Ch 10.2
sunflower Ch 12, Ch 12.2
Suresh Kumar Sharma Ch 3
surveillance cameras Ch 7.3
Sus Ch 10.3, Ch 13.4
swim Ch 3
swirling galaxies Ch 12
Sydney Ch 11.3
synchronicity Ch 14.2
synthetic life forms Ch 9.2
T-shirts Ch 3
Tablets Ch 8.3
Tagalog Ch 13.3
Taj Mahal Ch 4
tallest man Ch 3
Tang Dynasty Ch 10.2
tardigrades Ch 3.1, Ch 9
tattoos Ch 3
Technology Ch 8
technophobes Ch 10.2
Telemedicine Platforms Ch 8.3
Terabit Speeds Ch 3.3
Terminator, The Ch 1.2
Tesla, Nikola Ch 9.2, Ch 10
Text Messaging (SMS) Ch 8.3
Thailand Ch 6, Ch 6.1
the bee's knees Ch 13.4
therapists Ch 7.2
Thermostats, Smart Ch 8.3
Thingamajig Ch 6.2, Ch 13.1
Thirty Years' War, The Ch 10.2
Tierra del Fuego Ch 13.3
Tim Berners-Lee Ch 3.2
time capsule Ch 4
time dilation Ch 7.1
Time Machine, The Ch 7.3
time travel Ch 7.1, Ch 7.3
tines Ch 2.3, Ch 13.2
Tinku festival Ch 6.1
Titanic Ch 1.2
Titanic, RMS Ch 14.1
tittle Ch 2.3, Ch 13.2
Tom Selleck Ch 1.2
tomatoes Ch 6.1
tomorrow Ch 2.3, Ch 13.2
toothbrush Ch 1.3

Toronto, Ontario, Canada Ch 12.2
tortoise Ch 3.1
Trampoline gymnastics Ch 11.3
Treaty of Tordesillas Ch 10.2
tri-capital Ch 4
triple point Ch 5.3
Tristan da Cunha Ch 4.1
Tshirts Ch 3
tug-of-war Ch 11.3
Tulsishyam Hill in the Gir Forest Ch 5
Moncton, Canada   Ch 5.2
turbulence Ch 12.1
Turing, Alan Ch 8
Turkmenistan Ch 5.2
turtles Ch 5.3
U.S. Navy Ch 10
ubuntu Ch 13.3
uciferin Ch 5
Uckers Ch 11.2
Ultimate Frisbee Ch 11.3
underwater ironing Ch 11.1
United Nations building, The Ch 12.2
United States Ch 4
urine Ch 5.3
USB Flash Drives Ch 8.3
Utah Ch 5.2
vaccines Ch 3.2
vacuum of space Ch 3.1
vagitus Ch 2.3, Ch 13.2
Vatican City Ch 4
vegetarianism Ch 2.2
Velcro Ch 10
Venus Ch 5.3
VHS tapes Ch 7.3
viceroy butterfly Ch 9
Victorian dinner party Ch 2.2
Vietnam Ch 5.2
Vikings, The Ch 11.2
Vint Cerf Ch 3.2
violin Ch 7.2
viral videos Ch 1.1
Virgin Galactic Ch 8.2
virtual assistant Ch 3.3, Ch 8, Ch 8.1
virtual environments Ch 7.2
Visual art Ch 12
Vitruvian Man Ch 12.2

vocables Ch 2.3, Ch 13.2
volcano Ch 3.1
vomitorium Ch 2.2
Voyager Ch 3.2
VR Ch 7.2
VR headsets Ch 7.2
Wadlow, Robert Ch 3
Waffle the Warrior Cat Ch 3.1
Waitomo Caves Ch 5.2
Wales Ch 6.1
Walkman Ch 8.3
Wall Street Journal, The Ch 11.1
wamble Ch 2.3, Ch 13.2
Warren G. Harding Ch 14.1
Wartime cooking Ch 2.2
Washington D.C. Ch 10.1, Ch 10.2
water bear Ch 3.1, Ch 9
Water Bottles, Reusable Ch 8.3
Watson Ch 7.2
Wave, a rock formation, The Ch 5.2
Weakly Interacting Massive Particles (WIMPs) Ch 9.1
webcam Ch 7.3
wedding veil Ch 5.3
Wells, H.G. Ch 7.3
Wendy's Ch 2
Western Australia Ch 5.2
WFPC2 Ch 3.2
WhatchamacallitCh 6.2, Ch 13.1
Whippersnapper Ch 6.2, Ch 13.1
whitewater Ch 11.3
Wi-Fi Ch 7.3, Ch 8.3
Wi-Fi technology Ch 10
Wide Field and Planetary Camera 2 (WFPC2) Ch 3.2
Will Smith Ch 1.2
William Gibson Ch 7.3
William Henry Harrison Ch 14.1
William McKinley Ch 14.1
Williams, Hugh Ch 14.2
Willis Carrier Ch 10
WIMPs Ch 9.1
wind turbines Ch 3.3
windshield wipers Ch 10
Winslet, Kate Ch 1.2
Wireless Charging Pads Ch 8.3

wireless charging technologies Ch 10
wireless communication Ch 10
wireless energy transfer Ch 10
Wisconsin Ch 6
Wombat Ch 5.3
World Bog Snorkeling Championship Ch 6.1
World of Extreme Ironing, The Ch 11.1
World War I Ch 10.2
World War I veterans Ch 10.2
World War II Ch 10
World Wide Web Ch 8.3
World's Fair Ch 2
wormholes Ch 7.1
Wreck of the Titan, The Ch 14.1
Xilxes Ch 6.1
Yaghan Ch 13.3
Yahtzee Ch 11.2
Yemen Ch 4.1
Yule Lads Ch 6.1
Zanzibar Ch 5.3
Zeus, the Great Dane Ch 3.1
Ziegland, Henry Ch 14.2
zugzwang Ch 13
φ (phi) Ch 12.2

Thank you once again for being an incredible part of this journey. Keep exploring, keep questioning,
and most importantly, keep laughing. Until our next adventure!

References

10 Group Trivia Games that are Super Fun (And Mostly Free) https://slideswith.com/blog/group-trivia-games

10 Oddest Food Laws From Around The World https://www.mashed.com/1257738/oddest-food-laws-around-world/

12 English words with truly strange origins - EF Education First https://www.ef.edu/blog/language/english-words-with-strange-origins/

120 True Or False Questions To Use In Your Next Quiz https://games4esl.com/true-or-false-questions/

18 Best Trivia Games & Activities For Adults https://teambuilding.com/blog/trivia-for-adults

20 Unusual (& Weird) Festivals Around the World https://www.headout.com/blog/unusual-festivals-in-the-world/

28 Untranslatable Words from Around the World https:// ourworldenglish.com/28-untranslatable-words-from-around-the- world/

28 Weird Wedding Rituals From Around The World https://www. larsonjewelers.com/pages/28-weird-wedding-rituals-from- around-the-world?srsltid=AfmBOooJoXliLmyX- Kl6PnyfSSvP1nAAH-8w2r14BVSH-f_08QZviw2N

31 Crazy Behind-the-Scenes Facts About Our Favorite Movies ... https://trivia.cracked.com/image-pictofact-8723-31-crazy- behind-the-scenes-facts-about-our-favorite-movies-and-tv- shows

32 sci-fi technology predictions that came true https://www. livescience.com/technology/sci-fi-technology-predictions-that- came-true

39 Fun Facts About World Capitals https://traveltriviachallenge. com/fun-facts-about-world-capitals/

7 ethically controversial research areas in science and ... https:// interestingengineering.com/science/7-ethically-controversial- research-areas-in-science-and-technology

7 Quirky—and Discontinued —Summer Olympic Events https:// www.history.com/news/olympic-events-discontinued

7 Strange Geological Phenomena You Won't Believe Exist https:// geologyscience.com/gallery/geologic-lists/7-strange-geological- phenomena-you-wont-believe-exist/?amp

8 Famous Monuments That Are Hiding Little-Known Secrets https://www.rd.com/list/monument-secrets/

"Alberts, B., et al. (2015). Molecular biology of the cell (6th ed.). Garland Science."

"Anaya, C. (2022, October 22). The candy that almost ended up in E.T., and why it didn't. The Daily Meal. https://www.thedailymeal.com/entertainment/candy-almost-ended-et"

Artificial Intelligence and the Future of Space Exploration https://ai-solutions.com/newsroom/about-us/news-multimedia/artificial-intelligence-and-the-future-of-space-exploration/

"Atlas Obscura. (n.d.). Electric Brae: Scotland's gravity-defying road. Atlas Obscura. Retrieved June 17, 2024, from https://www.atlasobscura.com"

Australian Koala Foundation. (2020). Koala facts. https://www.savethekoala.com

"BBC News. (2018, August 15). Garden gnome sanctuary brings smiles to Devon. BBC News. Retrieved from https://www.bbc.co.uk/news"

"Beech, M. (2016). Why cats can't taste sweetness. Journal of Animal Physiology, 41(6), 592-597."

"Bell, T. (1962). The origins of the modem. IEEE Transactions on Communication, 10(3), 59-63. https://doi.org/10.1109/TCOM.1962.1093310"

Benoît Lecomte https://en.wikipedia.org/wiki/Beno%C3%AEt_Lecomte

Berry Patch Farms. (n.d.). Do shrimp have hearts? Retrieved from https://www.berrypatchfarms.net

Beverage Can Makers America. (2021). The history of the beverage can. Beverage Can Makers America. https://www.beveragecans.org/history

"Bonan, G. B. (2018). Amazon rainforest: The lungs of the Earth. Journal of Climate Science. https://doi.org/10.1175/JCLI-D-17-0878.1"

"Bowers, D. (2012). The soda can: A history of the beverage container. University of Arizona Press."

"Brackett, M. (2017). The longest hiccuping spree in history. Guinness World Records. https://www.guinnessworldrecords.com"

"Brown, M. (2016). Kevlar: The story of the strong synthetic fiber. DuPont Innovation Press. Retrieved from https://www.dupont.com/kevlar.html"

"Buchanan, R. (2019). World's shortest flight: The 57-second journey in the Orkney Islands. BBC Travel. https://www.bbc.com"

"Bushdid, C., et al. (2014). Humans can detect thousands of scents. Science, 343(6177), 1370-1371. https://doi.org/10.1126/science.1245990"

camouflage - National Geographic Education https://education.nationalgeographic.org/resource/camouflage

"Campbell, D. (2017). How much does a cloud weigh? National Weather Service. https://www.weather.gov"

"Carmichael, L. (2018). The science of humming and why you can't hum with your nose closed. Psychology Today. https://www.psychologytoday.com"

"Carter, C. (2014). The history and evolution of beverage packaging. Packaging Technology and Science, 27(9), 642-654. https://doi.org/10.1002/pts.2009"

CBS. (n.d.). NCIS Gibbs' rules: Complete list. Retrieved from https://www.cbs.com

"Chakrabarti, S. (2020, May 8). The Matrix: A franchise built on alternate realities, science fiction, and symbolism. Screen Rant. https://screenrant.com/the-matrix-franchise-reality-symbolism-facts/"

"Comer, D. E. (2006). Internetworking with TCP/IP: Volume 1, Principles, protocols, and architecture (6th ed.). Pearson Education."

Commonplace Fun Facts. (2022). How E.T. made Reese's Pieces one of the world's favorite candies. Commonplace Facts. https://commonplacefacts.com/et-reese-pieces/

"Cookist. (2023, August 28). What is La Tomatina Festival and how many tomatoes are wasted during it? Cookist. https://www.cookist.com/la-tomatina-festival-2023"

"Crowther, T. W., Glick, H. R., Lavers, J. L., & Turner, B. L. (2015). Mapping tree density across the globe. Nature, 525(7568), 211-215. https://doi.org/10.1038/nature14967"

"Dark matter | Definition, Discovery, Distribution, & Facts https://www.britannica.com/science/dark-matter"

"Debczak, M. (2017, June 29). It's illegal to own only one guinea pig in Switzerland. Mental Floss. Retrieved from https://www.mentalfloss.com"

Decoding the Secret Symbolism in Famous ... https://www.invaluable.com/blog/decoding-the-secret-symbolism-in-famous-paintings/?srsltid=AfmBOoqAwOs_JpTU0aupoekx7fjoJiTK_p GN_qwe6LRslupokMEerJDV

"Discover India. (n.d.). Magnetic Hill in Ladakh: Mystery or illusion? Retrieved June 17, 2024, from https://www.discoverindia.in"

Divine Proportion/Golden Ratio in the Art of Da Vinci https://www.goldennumber.net/leonardo-da-vinci-golden-ratio-art/

"Dupont, S. K. (2014). The accidental invention of Kevlar: Stephanie Kwolek's contribution to material science. DuPont Research Archives. Retrieved from https://www.dupont.com/science/kevlar-history.html"

"El País. (2022, November 7). The night the crew of 'Titanic' was drugged with angel dust in their soup. Retrieved from https://english.elpais.com/culture/2022-11-07/the-night-the-crew-of-titanic-was-drugged-with-angel-dust-in-their-soup.html"

"English in Pop Culture: The Language of Music, Movies ... https://www.park.edu/blog/english-in-pop-culture-the-language-of-music-movies-and-tv-shows/"

Extreme ironing https://en.wikipedia.org/wiki/Extreme_ironing

Fact check: 1964 Lincoln-Kennedy list is only partly accurate https://www.usatoday.com/story/news/factcheck/2020/06/06/fact-check-1964-lincoln-kennedy-comparisons-only-partly-accurate/5311926002/

"Farber, D. (1997). The history of the 56K modem. IEEE Spectrum, 34(4), 54-60. https://ieeexplore.ieee.org/document/589407"

Fibonacci sequence https://en.wikipedia.org/wiki/Fibonacci_sequence

Film School Rejects. (2023). The sound design secrets of Jurassic Park: Creating dinosaur roars. Retrieved from https://filmschoolrejects.com

"Foucault, M. (2004). Mona Lisa and the mystery of her missing eyebrows. Art History Today. https://www.arthistorytoday.com"

"Fraze, E. (1962). Patent for a can with a pull-tab opening. U.S. Patent No. 3,097,427."

Geological Formations That Baffle Scientists https://www.mentalfloss.com/article/609355/geological-formations-baffle-scientists

"Gill, S. (2015). Why honey doesn't spoil. Smithsonian. https://www.smithsonianmag.com/science-nature/why-honey-doesnt-spoil-180953428/"

"Global News. (2022, November 11). Titanic, PCP and chowder: New details about drugging on 1996 film set in Halifax revealed. Retrieved from https://globalnews.ca/news/9187918/titanic-crew-drugged-chowder-james-cameron-hospital"

"Gnome Reserve and Wildflower Garden. (n.d.). Visit the Gnome Reserve. Retrieved June 17, 2024, from http://www.gnomereserve.co.uk"

"Goodwin, J., & Jensen, H. (2018). Polymer chemistry and the development of Kevlar. Journal of Polymer Science, 56(2), 134-145. https://doi.org/10.1002/pol.2018.01"

"Goody, J. (1998). The development of the family and marriage in Europe. Cambridge University Press."

"Guinness World Records. (2005). Longest cat whiskers. Guinness World Records. Retrieved June 17, 2024, from https://www.guinnessworldrecords.com"

"Guinness World Records. (2013). Longest kiss: 58 hours, 35 minutes and 58 seconds. Guinness World Records. Retrieved June 17, 2024, from https://www.guinnessworldrecords.com"

"Guinness World Records. (2014, July 17). Kemps celebrates 100th anniversary with largest ice cream scoop. Retrieved from https://www.guinnessworldrecords.com"

"Guinness World Records. (2014). Fastest tortoise. Guinness World Records. Retrieved June 17, 2024, from https://www.guinnessworldrecords.com"

"Guinness World Records. (2017). Largest gathering of people dressed as penguins. Guinness World Records. Retrieved June 17, 2024, from https://www.guinnessworldrecords.com"

Guinness World Records. (2018). Longest bridal veil. Guinness World Records. https://www.guinnessworldrecords.com

"Guinness World Records. (2020). Longest ears on a dog (living). Guinness World Records. Retrieved June 17, 2024, from https://www.guinnessworldrecords.com"

"Guinness World Records. (2021, September 22). Lou the coonhound breaks record for longest ears on a dog. Guinness World Records. Retrieved June 17, 2024, from https://www. guinnessworldrecords.com"

"Guinness World Records. (2022). Longest duration spinning a basketball on a toothbrush. Guinness World Records. Retrieved June 17, 2024, from https://www.guinnessworldrecords.com"

"Guinness World Records. (2023, January 27). YouTuber Airrack claims slice of history with world's largest pizza. Retrieved from https://www.guinnessworldrecords.com"

"Guinness World Records. (n.d.). Largest collection of garden gnomes and pixies. Guinness World Records. Retrieved June 17, 2024, from https://www.guinnessworldrecords.com"

"Guinness World Records. (n.d.). Magnetic Hill, Moncton: The illusion that defies gravity. Guinness World Records. Retrieved June 17, 2024, from https://www.guinnessworldrecords.com"

Hafthor Bjornsson breaks world record with 1104-pound ... https://www.espn.com/olympics/weightlifting/story/_/id/ 29126863/hafthor-bjornsson-breaks-world-record-501-kilogram- deadlift

"Hargrove, T. (2021). Impact resistance and material properties of Kevlar: How it works. Materials Today, 24(8), 56-63. https://doi. org/10.1016/j.mattod.2021.04.002"

"Hendricks, G. (2015). The science of fruit: Pineapples explained. National Geographic. https://www.nationalgeographic.com"

"Houghton, M. (2016). Why bananas are berries and strawberries are not. The New York Times. https://www.nytimes.com"

How does bioluminescence work? https://www.whoi.edu/know-your-ocean/did-you-know/how-does-bioluminescence-work/

How Hollywood Star Hedy Lamarr Invented the Tech ... https://www.history.com/news/hedy-lamarr-inventor-frequency-hopping-wifi

How To Rule Your Own Country: The Outrageous World Of ... https://www.forbes.com/sites/jimdobson/2023/09/21/how-to-rule-your-own-country-inside-the-outrageous-world-of-micronations/

"Howard, D. (2019). The origins of the first computer virus. Computer History Museum. https://www.computerhistory.org"

"Hubble Space Telescope Science Institute. (1993, December 6). Hubble's first servicing mission: Correcting the primary mirror flaw. Space Telescope Science Institute. https://hubblesite.org/contents/news-releases/1993/news-1993-06"

IMDb. (n.d.). NCIS (TV series): Gibbs' rules. Retrieved from https://www.imdb.com

Innovative architecture in the age of Justinian (article) https://www.khanacademy.org/humanities/medieval-world/byzantine1/x4b0eb531:early-byzantine-including-iconoclasm/a/innovative-architecture-in-the-age-of-justinian

"Interesting Facts. (n.d.). In Switzerland, it is illegal to own just one guinea pig. Retrieved from https://www.interestingfacts.com"

Internet meme https://en.wikipedia.org/wiki/Internet_meme

Is Time Travel Possible? https://www.scientificamerican.com/article/is-time-travel-possible/

"Joshi, S. (2023, January 23). The world's largest pizza ever made in Los Angeles. Food and Beverage Insider. Retrieved from https://www.foodbeverageinsider.com"

"Kearney, A. (2019). Why wombats produce cube-shaped poop. Australian Geographic. https://www.australiangeographic.com.au"

Kemps Dairy. (2014). Largest ice cream scoop world record set by Kemps. Retrieved from https://www.kemps.com

"Lass, D. D. (2003). Broadband technologies: DSL and cable modems. Journal of Telecommunications and Information Technology, 5, 29-34."

"Leclair, A. (2018). Giraffes: The silent giants of the animal kingdom. National Geographic. https://www.nationalgeographic.com"

Leskin, Paige. "How a cat named Smudge's distaste for salad created one of 2019's most popular memes". Business Insider.

List of common misconceptions https://en.wikipedia.org/wiki/List_of_common_misconceptions

"Livingstone, D. N. (2014). Geography and geographers: Anglo-American human geography since 1945 (7th ed.). Routledge."

Mad Science: Nine of the oddest experiments ever https://www.newscientist.com/article/dn14801-mad-science-nine-of-the-oddest-experiments-ever/

Maddog. (n.d.). Arnold's lines in The Terminator. Massachusetts Institute of Technology. Retrieved from https://people.csail.mit.edu/maddog/terminator.html

Major Accomplishments of NASA's Voyager 1 and 2 Spacecraft https://scitechdaily.com/major-accomplishments-of-nasas-voyager-1-and-2-spacecraft/

"Mathews, M. (2002). The digital revolution: From 56K modems to fiber optics. Communications of the ACM, 45(8), 47-51. https://doi.org/10.1145/514236.514242"

"Mattingly, L. (2016). How similar are humans and bananas? Science Daily. https://www.sciencedaily.com"

Mature and Old-Growth Forests https://www.fs.usda.gov/managing-land/old-growth-forests

"McCall, M. (2015). Astronomers discover planet made mostly of diamond. Science News. https://www.sciencenews.org"

"McGhee, G. R. (2018). The evolution of the shark. Oxford University Press."

"McKnight, T. L., & Hess, D. (2017). Physical geography: A landscape appreciation (12th ed.). Pearson Education."

"Mental Floss. (n.d.). 2000s Slang: 30 Amazeballs Terms You Should Know. Retrieved November 10, 2024, from https://www.mentalfloss.com"

"Miller, A. (2020). Animal collective nouns: A flamboyance of flamingos. National Geographic. https://www.nationalgeographic.com"

"Mr. Boss Cat. (n.d.). Cat breeds with long whiskers. Mr. Boss Cat. Retrieved June 17, 2024, from https://mrbosscat.com"

"Murdock, G. P. (1949). Social structure. Macmillan."

Napoleon's defeat at Waterloo caused in part by ... https://phys.org/news/2018-08-napoleon-defeat-waterloo-indonesian-volcanic.html

"NASA. (1993, December 2). Hubble Space Telescope Servicing Mission (STS-61). NASA. https://www.nasa.gov/mission_pages/hubble/servicing/1993/sts61.html"

NASA. (2002). Hubble Space Telescope: A decade of discovery. NASA. https://www.nasa.gov/mission_pages/hubble/mission/index.html

NASA. (2017). How comets' tails are formed. NASA. https://www.nasa.gov

NASA. (2017). Why astronauts grow taller in space. NASA. https://www.nasa.gov

NASA. (2019). Venus facts. NASA. https://www.nasa.gov/venus-facts

NASA. (2020). Saturn facts. NASA. https://www.nasa.gov

NASA. (2020). Venus facts. NASA. https://www.nasa.gov/venus-facts

National Earth Sciences Institute. (2019). Earth's day length: The effects of rotation. https://www.nesi.org

National Earth Sciences Institute. (2020). Earth's slowing rotation and its impact. https://www.nesi.org

National Geographic Society. (n.d.). Geology. Retrieved from https://www.nationalgeographic.org

"National Geographic. (2021). The optical illusions of gravity hills. National Geographic. Retrieved June 17, 2024, from https://www.nationalgeographic.com"

National Zoo & Aquarium. (2020). Giant panda eating habits. Smithsonian. https://www.si.edu

"Nordine, M. (n.d.). Why it's illegal to own a single guinea pig in Switzerland. Retrieved from https://www.thelocal.ch"

Paleontology World. (n.d.). How they designed the T-Rex roar in Jurassic Park. Retrieved from https://paleontologyworld.com

"Pango Vet. (n.d.). World records for longest cat whiskers. Pango Vet. Retrieved June 17, 2024, from https://pangovet.com"

"Panksepp, J., & Burgdorf, J. (2003). Laughing rats and the evolutionary origins of human joy. Physiology & Behavior, 79(3), 459-468. https://doi.org/10.1016/S0031-9384(03)00123-X"

"Parker, H. (2017). Ancient Roman hygiene and its oddities. The History Channel. https://www.history.com"

"Phipps, K. (2015, October 21). The evolution of the Back to the Future time machine from refrigerator to DeLorean. The A.V. Club. Retrieved from https://www.avclub.com"

"Pizza Margherita - Wikipedia https://en.wikipedia.org/wiki/Pizza_Margherita#:~:text=History,-Pizzeria%20de'%20Figli-

ole&text=A%20popular%20contemporary%20le-
gend%20holds,of%20the%20visit-
ing%20Queen%20Margherita."

"Provides an in-depth look at the history and technical aspects of data communications, covering modem speeds, DSL, cable modems, and fiber-optic networks."

Pull or Push? Octopuses Solve a Puzzle Problem - PMC https://www.ncbi.nlm.nih.gov/pmc/articles/PMC4803207/

"Reader's Digest. (2022). Slang Words We Love from 2022. Retrieved November 10, 2024, from https://www.rd.com"

"Reader's Digest. (2023). New Slang Words You'll Be Hearing More of in 2023. Retrieved November 10, 2024, from https://www.rd.com"

Reynolds Metals Company. (1975). Stay-on-tab: A new innovation in can design. Reynolds Metals Company.

"Ripley's Believe It or Not!. (2013). Thai couple breaks the world record for the longest kiss. Ripley's Believe It or Not! Retrieved June 17, 2024, from https://www.ripleys.com"

"Roberts, E. A. (1999). The making of the English peasantry: The historical roots of the modern family. Routledge."

"Roff, W. A. (2016). The Anglo-Zanzibar war: The shortest war in history. History Today. https://www.historytoday.com"

"Sanderson, M. (2016). Cows form friendships. The Guardian. https://www.theguardian.com"

Science Channel. (2017). Boiling and freezing at the same time: The triple point phenomenon. https://www.sciencechannel.com

"Seitz, M. Z. (2021, June 15). How The Shining influenced Toy Story. Vulture. Retrieved from https://www.vulture.com"

Shaykh Academy. (2024). Did you know? A shrimp's heart is located in its head. Retrieved from https://theshaykhacademy.com

"Shostak, S. (2017). The vastness of space: How many stars are there? SETI Institute. https://www.seti.org"

"Smith, R. M. (1993). Hubble Space Telescope's first servicing mission: Space shuttle Endeavour's STS-61 mission and the installation of corrective optics. Space Shuttle Program Office. https://www.nasa.gov/sites/default/files/atoms/files/hubble_1st_servicing_mission.pdf"

"Sreenivasan, P. (2009). Marriage customs in India: The role of dowries and gifts. In T. S. Ghosh & S. K. Pillai (Eds.), Rural economic development and social change (pp. 134-151). Sage Publications."

"Stallings, W. (2013). Data and computer communications (10th ed.). Pearson."

"Steinhart, E. (2019). The octopus: A multifaceted creature. National Geographic. https://www.nationalgeographic.com"

"Stern, A. (2006). Pluto: The reclassification of a planet. NASA. https://www.nasa.gov"

"Stoltz, B. (2017). Sloths: The surprising animal that holds its breath for up to 40 minutes. The Guardian. https://www.theguardian.com"

Strange Driving Laws from Around the World https://www.firsttimedriver.com/blog/strange-driving-laws/

"Symbolism in the Forbidden City: The Magnificent Design ... https://www.asianstudies.org/publications/eaa/archives/symbolism-in-the-forbidden-city-the-magnificent-design-distinct-colors-and-lucky-numbers-of-chinas-imperial-palace/#:~:text=Even%20the%20design%20of%20the,lived%20or%20-did%20important%20business."

The 10 Most Odd Guinness World Records of 2023 https://929thelake.com/the-10-most-odd-guinness-world-records-of-2023/

The 9 weirdest events at the 2024 Olympics https://www.advnture.com/features/the-9-weirdest-events-at-the-2024-olympics

The Battle of Talas (751 AD): Catalyst for the Exchange of ... https://medium.com/@managing2024/the-battle-of-talas-751-ad-catalyst-for-the-exchange-of-paper-technology-between-the-arab-120addee1ee0

The Biggest Problem in Mathematics Is Finally a Step ... https://www.scientificamerican.com/article/the-riemann-hypothesis-the-biggest-problem-in-mathematics-is-a-step-closer/

The Engineering Behind the Great Pyramids of Giza https://

interestingengineering.com/innovation/the-engineering-behind-the-great-pyramids-of-giza

The Ethics of AI in Monitoring and Surveillance https://www.niceactimize.com/blog/fmc-the-ethics-of-ai-in-monitoring-and-surveillance/

The Evolution of Slang https://www.theatlantic.com/technology/archive/2014/08/the-evolution-of-slang/375104/

The History of Artificial Intelligence https://sitn.hms.harvard.edu/flash/2017/history-artificial-intelligence/

The Kitchen Know-How. (n.d.). The curious case of the shrimp's heart: Uncovering the unique anatomy of everyone's favorite crustacean. Retrieved from https://www.thekitchenknowhow.com

"The Matrix and its pop culture impact, themes, and legacy https://www.syfy.com/syfy-wire/the-matrix-and-its-pop-culture-impact-themes-and-legacy"

"The Olive Press. (2024, November 6). 130,000 kilos of tomatoes ready for return of Spain's world-famous La Tomatina festival in Valencia. The Olive Press. https://www.theolivepress.es/spain-news/2024/11/06/130000-kilos-of-tomatoes-ready-for-return-of-spains-world-famous-la-tomatina-festival-in-valencia"

"The Sacred Canopy, The Mystical Powers Of Forests https://treeplantation.com/the-spiritual-power-of-forests.html"

The Simplest Math Problem Could Be Unsolvable https://www.scientificamerican.com/article/the-simplest-math-problem-could-be-unsolvable/

"The Uncanny Case of the Jim Twins, Two Estranged ... https://www.ripleys.com/stories/jim-twins"

"The Wreck of the Titan: Or, Futility https://en.wikipedia.org/wiki/The_Wreck_of_the_Titan:_Or,_Futility"

These 15 sci-fi books actually predicted the future https://www.businessinsider.com/books-predicted-future-sci-fi-2018-11

These 5 secret societies changed the world—from behind ... https://www.nationalgeographic.com/history/history-magazine/article/influencing-history-one-secret-handshake-at-a-time

This is how Ancient Romans would feast https://www.cnn.com/style/how-ancient-romans-feasted/index.html

"Thompson, S. (2019, October 17). Why the Back to the Future time machine was almost a fridge. Screen Rant. Retrieved from https://screenrant.com"

Top 12 Real-World AI Applications in Healthcare https://empeek.com/insights/top-ai-applications-in-healthcare/

Traditional Games from around the World https://www.whatdowedoallday.com/traditional-games/

"Trager, C. (2016). How heat affects the Eiffel Tower's height. Smithsonian Magazine. https://www.smithsonianmag.com"

"Travel Triangle. (2023). Gravity-defying magnetic hills around the world. Travel Triangle. Retrieved June 17, 2024, from https://traveltriangle.com"

TV Insider. (2024). Your guide to Gibbs' rules on NCIS. Retrieved from https://www.tvinsider.com

U.S. National Weather Service. (2020). Record-breaking snowflake size. National Weather Service. https://www.weather.gov

United States Geological Survey. (n.d.). What is geology?. Retrieved from https://www.usgs.gov

"Vice. (2022, November 11). Remembering when the Titanic crew ate PCP-spiked clam chowder. Retrieved from https://www.vice.com/en/article/bvmdna/titanic-pcp-chowder-incident"

"Walker, C. (2015). Ocean quahog clam: The secret to its longevity. Marine Life Journal. https://www.marinebiolife.com"

What Is the Grandfather Paradox of Time Travel? https://www.discovermagazine.com/the-sciences/what-is-the-grandfather-paradox-of-time-travel

What the Luddites Really Fought Against https://www.smithsonianmag.com/history/what-the-luddites-really-fought-against-264412/

What We Know About the Earliest History of Chocolate https://www.smithsonianmag.com/history/archaeology-chocolate-180954243/

"When and how did traditional ""breakfast foods"" (eggs/ ... https://www.reddit.com/r/AskHistorians/comments/jdea8o/when_and_how_did_traditional_breakfast_foods/"

"Wikipedia contributors. (2024, October 17). La Tomatina. Wikipedia. https://en.wikipedia.org/wiki/La_Tomatina"

Wikipedia. (2023). I'll be back. Retrieved from https://en.wikipedia.org

Wikipedia. (2019). Woman yelling at a cat

World Record Academy. (2014). World's largest ice cream scoop sets new record. Retrieved from https://www.worldrecordacademy.com

"World Record Academy. (2024, July 26). World's largest pizza, world record in Los Angeles, California. Retrieved from https://www.worldrecordacademy.org"

"Wozniak, J. (2018). The secret lives of turtles. National Geographic. https://www.nationalgeographic.com"

"Yoshida, M. (2018). Japan's museum of ""face rocks"" reveals natural oddities. Japan Times. https://www.japantimes.co.jp"

"YouTube. (2021). This is the dog with the longest ears! | Guinness World Records. Retrieved June 17, 2024, from https://www.youtube.com"

"Zhang, Z., & Yuan, Y. (2017). 5G technology and future wireless networks. Wireless Communications and Mobile Computing, 2017, 1-9. https://doi.org/10.1155/2017/3798345"

"Zhou, X., & Liu, H. (2018). The evolution of fiber-optic internet: From broadband to gigabit and beyond. Journal of Optical Communications and Networking, 10(5), 432-440. https://doi.org/10.1364/JOCN.10.000432"

www.ingramcontent.com/pod-product-compliance
Lightning Source LLC
Chambersburg PA
CBHW062054270326
41931CB00013B/3066